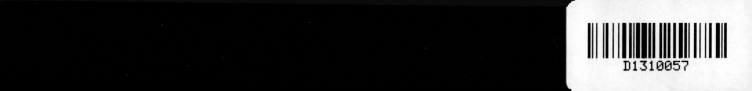

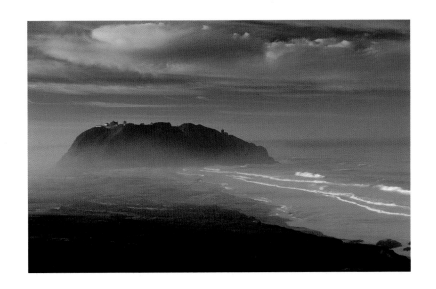

BIG SUR

and Beyond

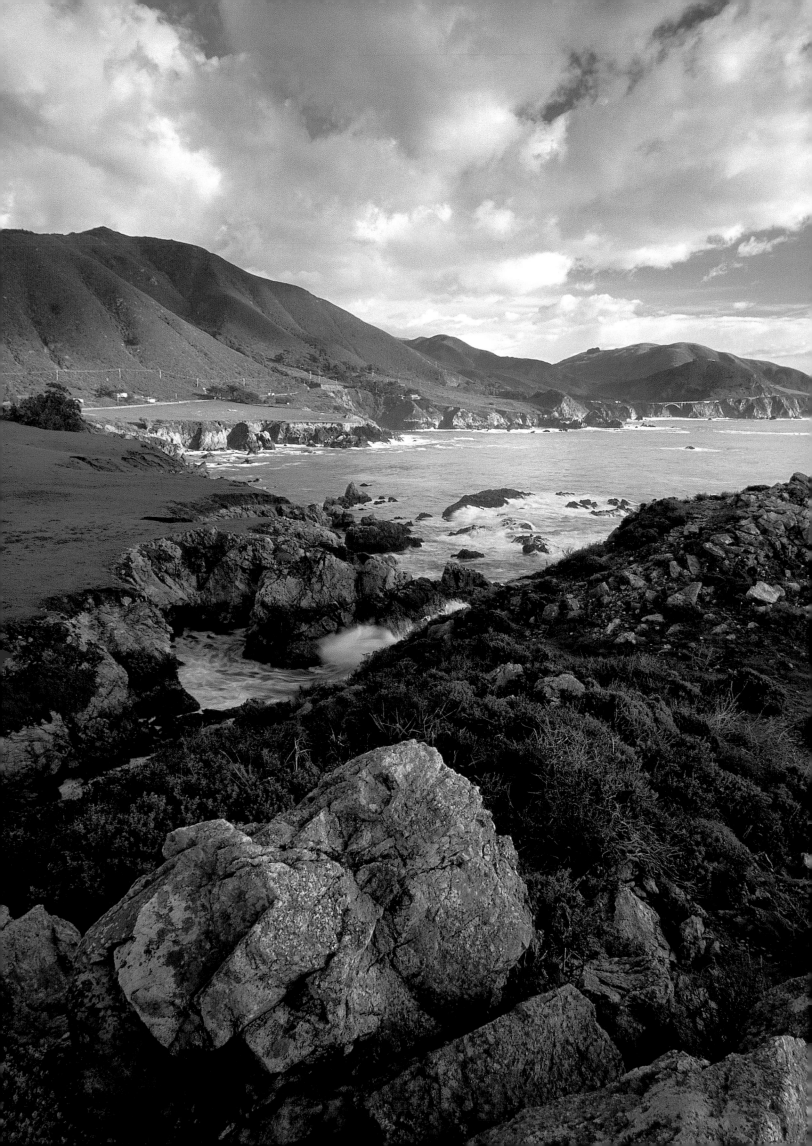

BIG SUR
and Beyond
THE LEGACY OF THE BIG SUR LAND TRUST

Photography by
DOUGLAS STEAKLEY

Foreword by
**CLINT EASTWOOD,
LEON PANETTA,
ROBERT REDFORD,**
and **TED TURNER**

Graphic Arts Center Publishing®

Library of Congress Cataloging-in-Publication Data
Steakley, Douglas, 1944–
  Big Sur and beyond : the legacy of the Big Sur Land Trust / photography by Douglas Steakley ; foreword by Clint Eastwood . . . [et al.].
    p. cm.
  ISBN 1-55868-609-6 (hardbound)
  1. Big Sur (Calif.)—Pictorial works. 2. Landscape—California—Big Sur—Pictorial works. 3. Natural history—California—Big Sur—Pictorial works.
4. Monterey County (Calif.)—Pictorial works. 5. Big Sur (Calif.)—Environmental conditions. 6. Monterey County (Calif.)—Environmental conditions. 7. Big Sur Land Trust. I. Title.
  F868.M7 S74 2001
  779'.36794'76—dc21
                                                             2001001871

President: Charles M. Hopkins
Associate Publisher: Douglas A. Pfeiffer
Editorial Staff: Timothy W. Frew, Ellen Harkins Wheat,
Tricia Brown, Kathy Matthews, Jean Andrews, Jean Bond-Slaughter
Production Staff: Richard L. Owsiany, Heather Doornink, Joanna Goebel
Cover Design: Elizabeth Watson
Interior Design: Jean Andrews
Map Makers: Nadene Torres and Stacy Dubuc
Printed in Hong Kong

Front cover and false title: El Sur Ranch and Point Sur from Highway 1.
Frontispiece and back cover: Rocky Point.
Front flap: Moonrise over Martin Dunes.
Facing page: Looking north from addition to Landels–Hill Big Creek Reserve.

CONTENTS

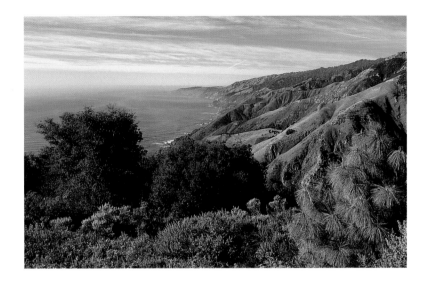

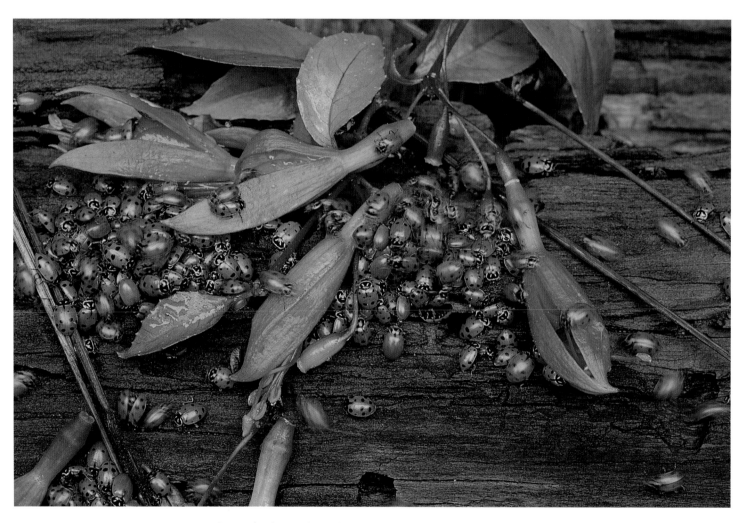

Above and right: Big Sur—home to living things large and small,
from towering redwoods to tiny ladybugs.
Overleaf: A storm moving over Big Sur's dramatic south coast.

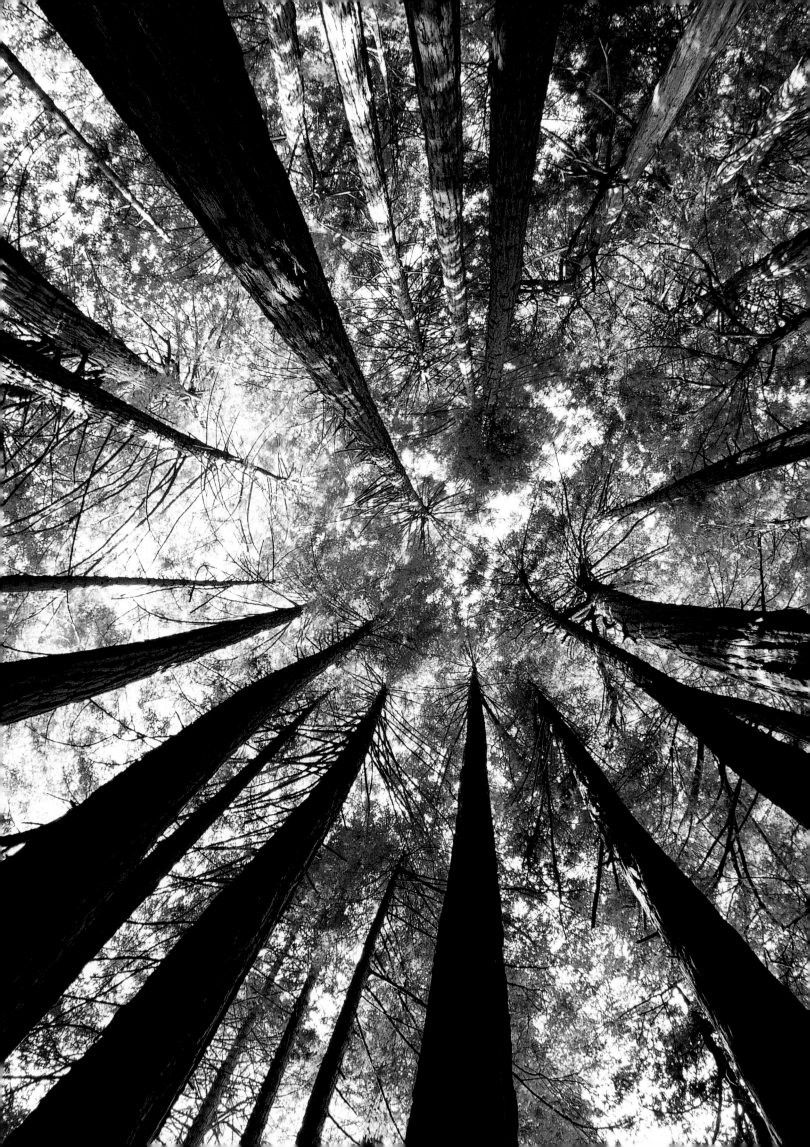

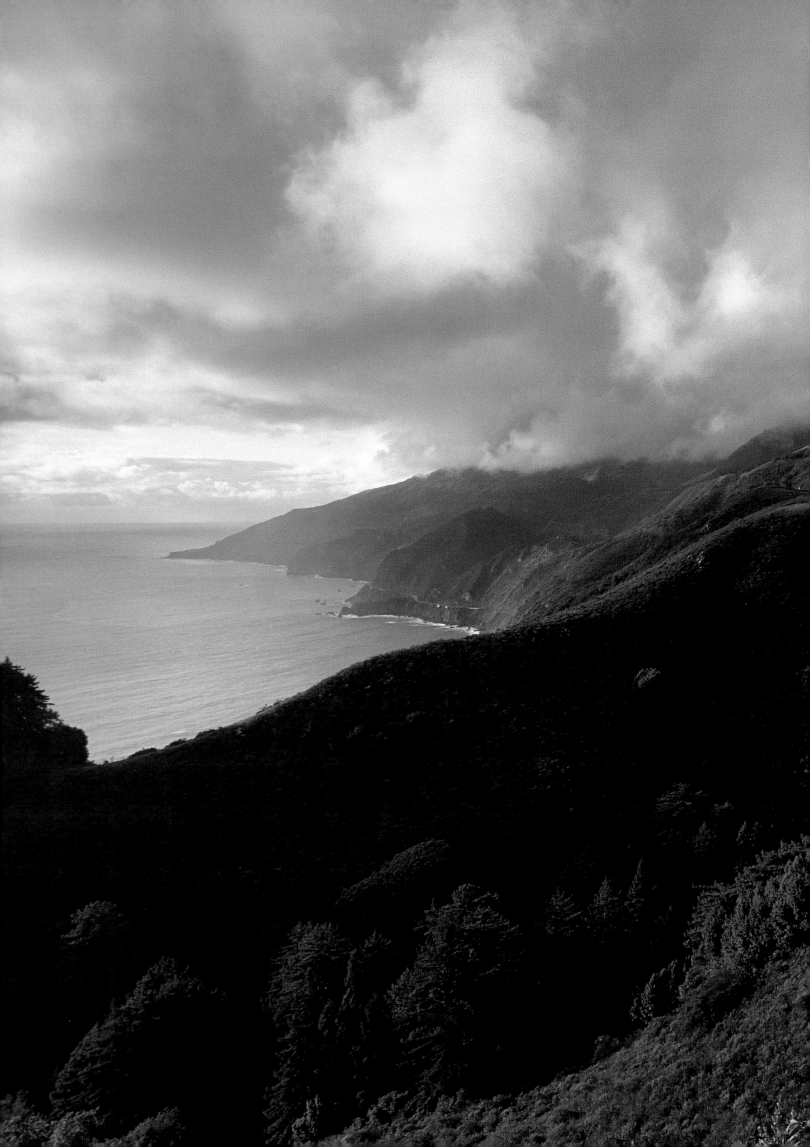

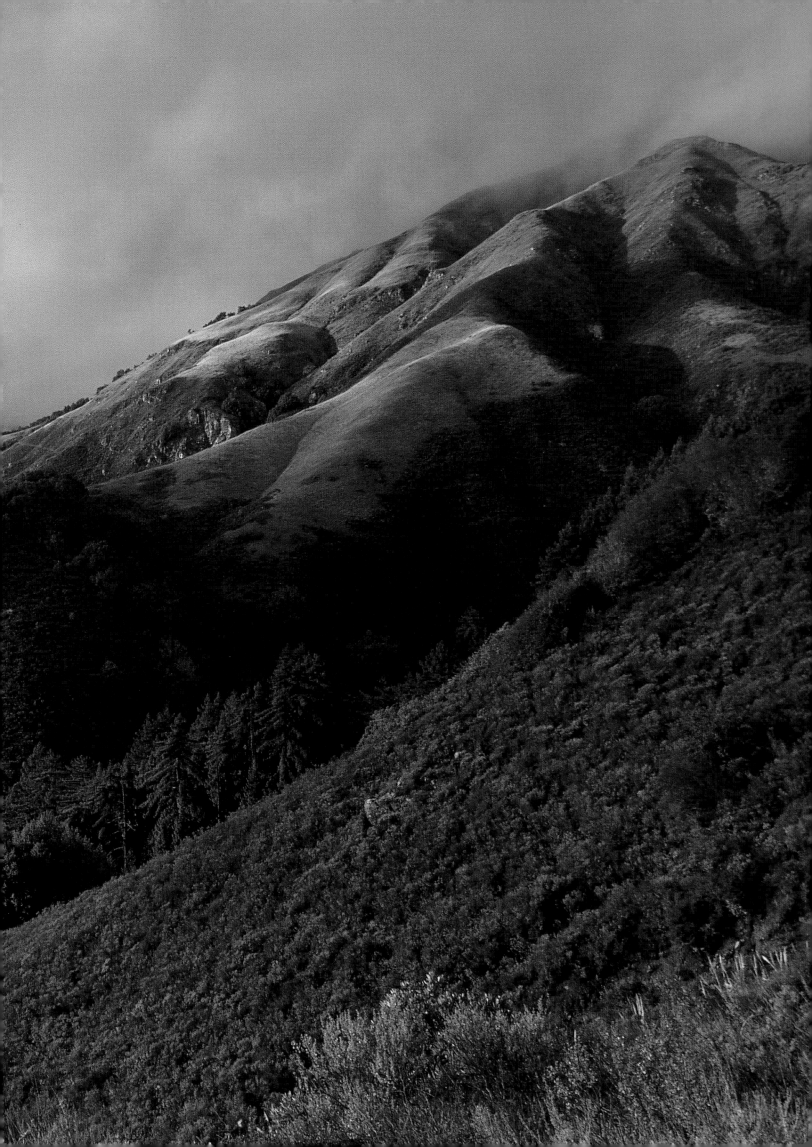

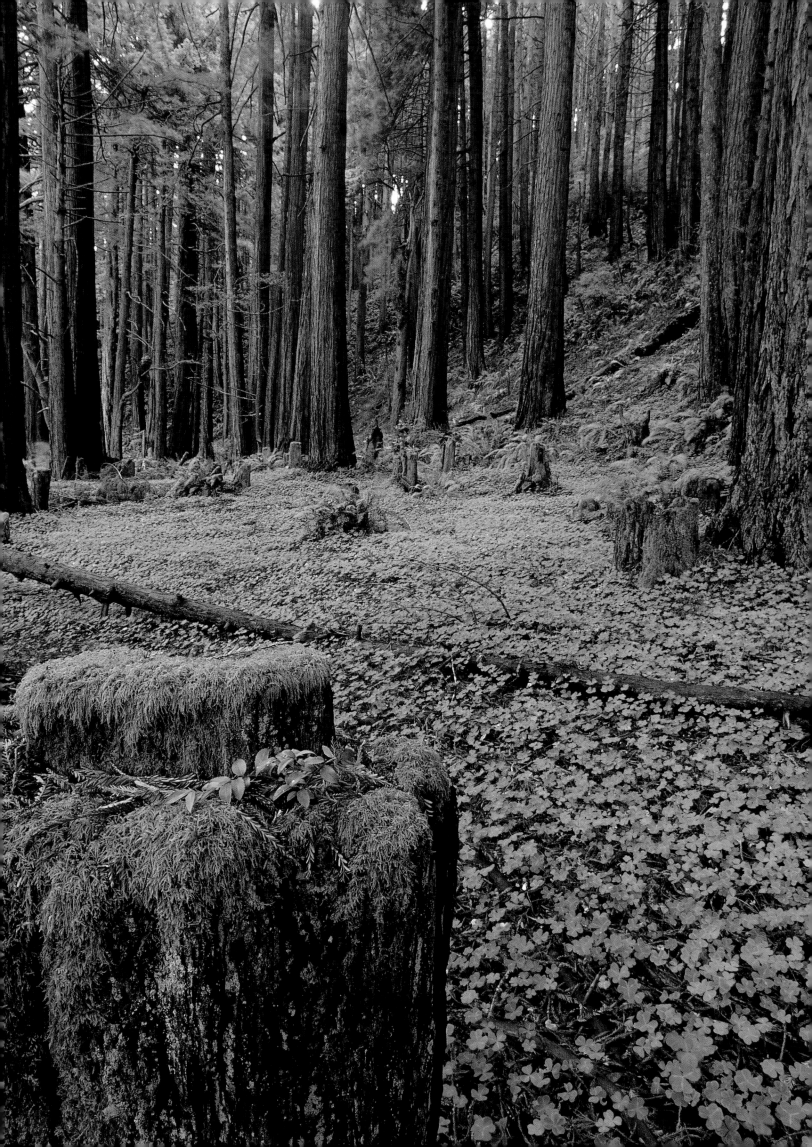

Foreword

THE BIG SUR LAND TRUST has worked for twenty-five years to preserve the spectacular lands of Big Sur and the Central California Coast. This worthy organization has gained national recognition and respect—and our strong, personal support—for its outstanding conservation efforts.

The mission of The Big Sur Land Trust is to protect for the public benefit those lands in Monterey County that are significant natural habitat, open space, agricultural, watershed, and recreational properties. Through the quiet and tireless efforts of its trustees, staff, and volunteers, The Big Sur Land Trust has preserved countless acres of irreplaceable lands in Big Sur and Monterey County.

A hundred years from now, future generations will enjoy the same spectacular views of ancient redwood forests, emerald hills, dark canyons, and the dramatic Big Sur Coast that we enjoy today. The following pages are graced with Douglas Steakley's inspiring photographs of these majestic lands.

Big Sur and Beyond is a fitting celebration of The Big Sur Land Trust's successes. Preserving land creates a timeless legacy. We urge you to strengthen this legacy by supporting The Big Sur Land Trust.

Join us in celebrating twenty-five years of preservation and the publication of *Big Sur and Beyond*.

Clint Eastwood

Robert Redford

Leon Panetta

Ted Turner

Left: Redwood sorrel in a clearing along the Old Coast Road.

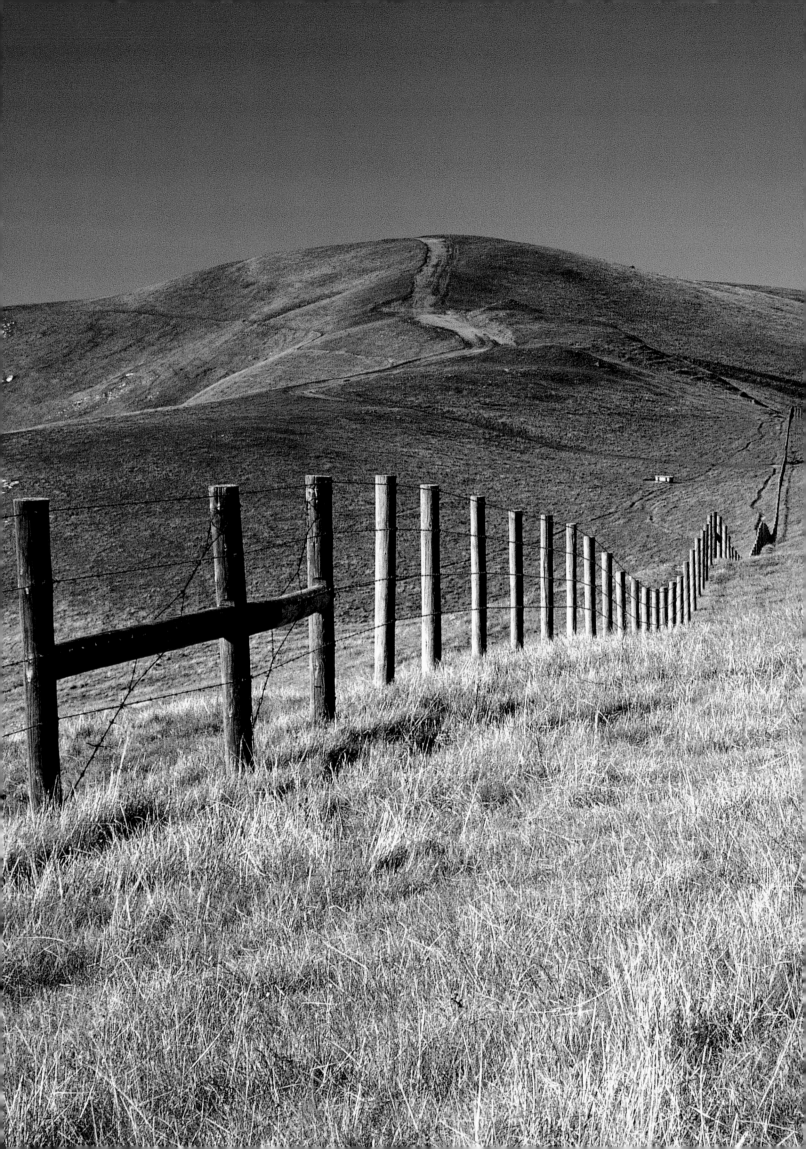

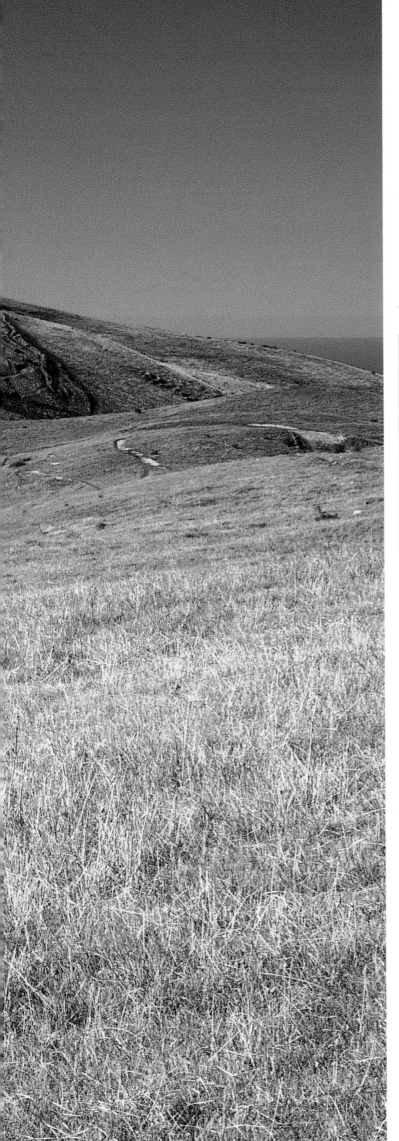

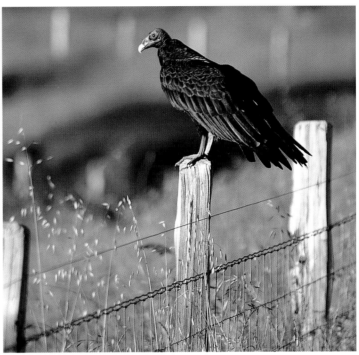

Left: Rolling coastal prairie on the El Sur Ranch,
as seen from the Bixby Ocean Ranch.
Above: A turkey vulture scanning the landscape.

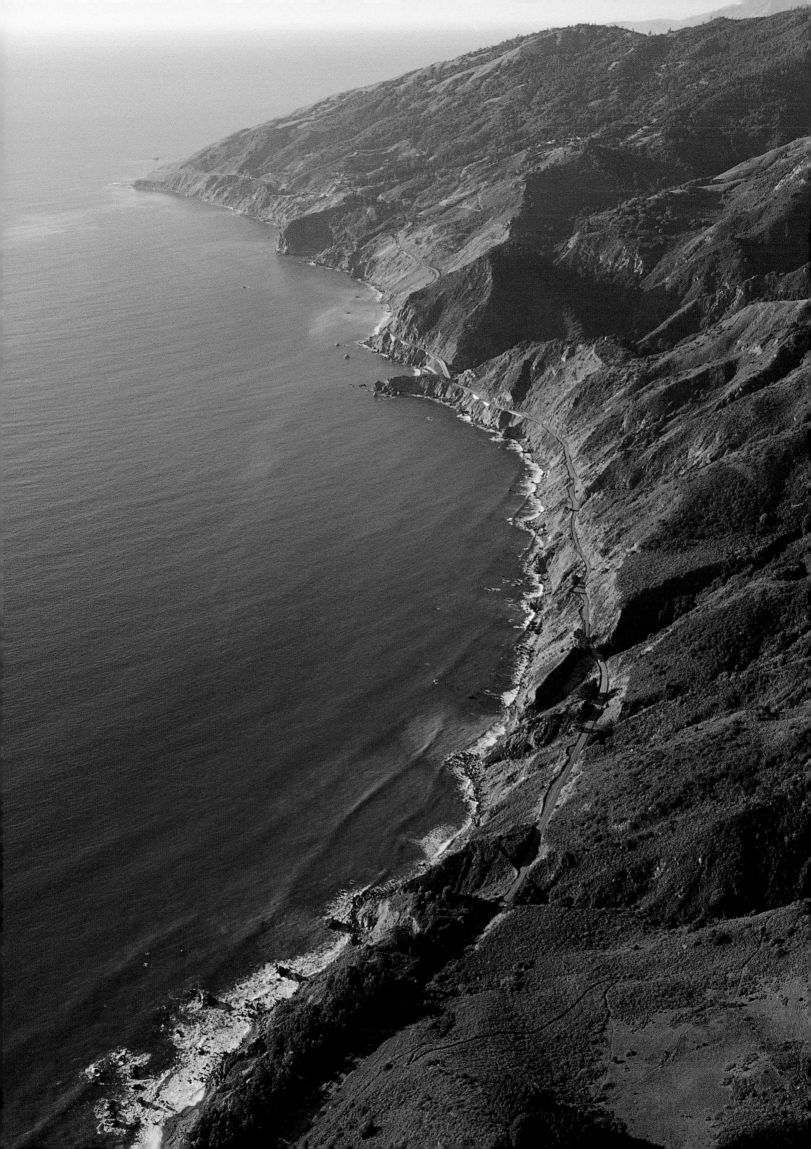

The Land and the Legacy

BIG SUR IS A PLACE of wild, unrivaled beauty, a dynamic meeting of mountain, sea, and sky. Here, among the redwoods and above the crashing waves of its spectacular coast, exists a harmonious but fragile balance between man and nature. Visitors come from around the world to experience the drama of mountains plunging into the waters of the Pacific Ocean, to enjoy abundant wildlife such as sea otters, migrating whales, mountain lions, and condors, and to stand in awe beside giant redwood trees.

Over the past quarter century, The Big Sur Land Trust has created a legacy of conservation through the acquisition of priority lands and the establishment of conservation easements. Through these efforts it is our goal to preserve these precious lands for generations to come.

Big Sur and Beyond tells the story of this conservation legacy through the eye of talented photographer Douglas Steakley. His generous donation of time and artistry have made this book possible. Douglas's inspiring photographs, depicting many of the rich land and wildlife resources protected by The Big Sur Land Trust, have influenced decision-makers and the public to conserve the irreplaceable natural heritage of Monterey County.

Established in 1978, The Big Sur Land Trust has protected more than twenty thousand acres of scenic, recreational, and wildlife lands. This charitable nonprofit organization works cooperatively with community groups, conservation organizations, private landowners, and public agencies to protect the biologically rich lands of the Big Sur Coast, the Monterey Bay State Seashore, Point Lobos, Carmel Valley, the Monterey Peninsula, the Elkhorn Slough Watershed, and other significant places.

This conservation legacy was made possible by the vision, hard work, and generosity of The Big Sur Land Trust's many public and private partners and the nearly two thousand Land Trust members worldwide.

Join with us in partnership as we work to build an even stronger conservation legacy so that future generations may enjoy the distinctive beauty of Big Sur and beyond. As we celebrate the first quarter century of conservation achievements, we must look forward to the increasing challenges ahead. California is growing dramatically and is poised to add the population of five cities the size of Los Angeles over the next few decades. Monterey County's population alone is expected to double, increasing the need to conserve irreplaceable open space. Preserving our natural resources will require increasing conservation commitment and action.

When you visit Big Sur and its surrounding areas, you are enjoying the spectacular vistas and rich environments protected by The Big Sur Land Trust. When you are at home or in your office, we hope this book provides continuing inspiration of nature's beauty and the assurance that, together, we can effectively protect our majestic natural landscapes.

—The Big Sur Land Trust

Left: The rugged terrain of Big Sur's south coast.

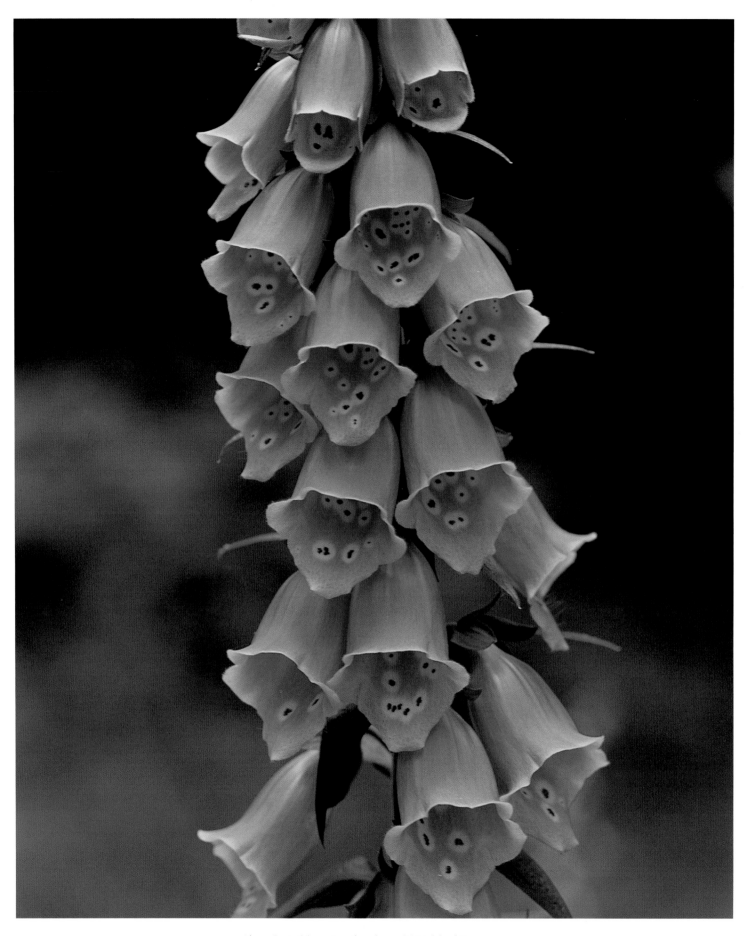

Above: Late-blooming foxglove, Mitteldorf Preserve.
Right: Cascading waterfall along Big Sur's south coast.

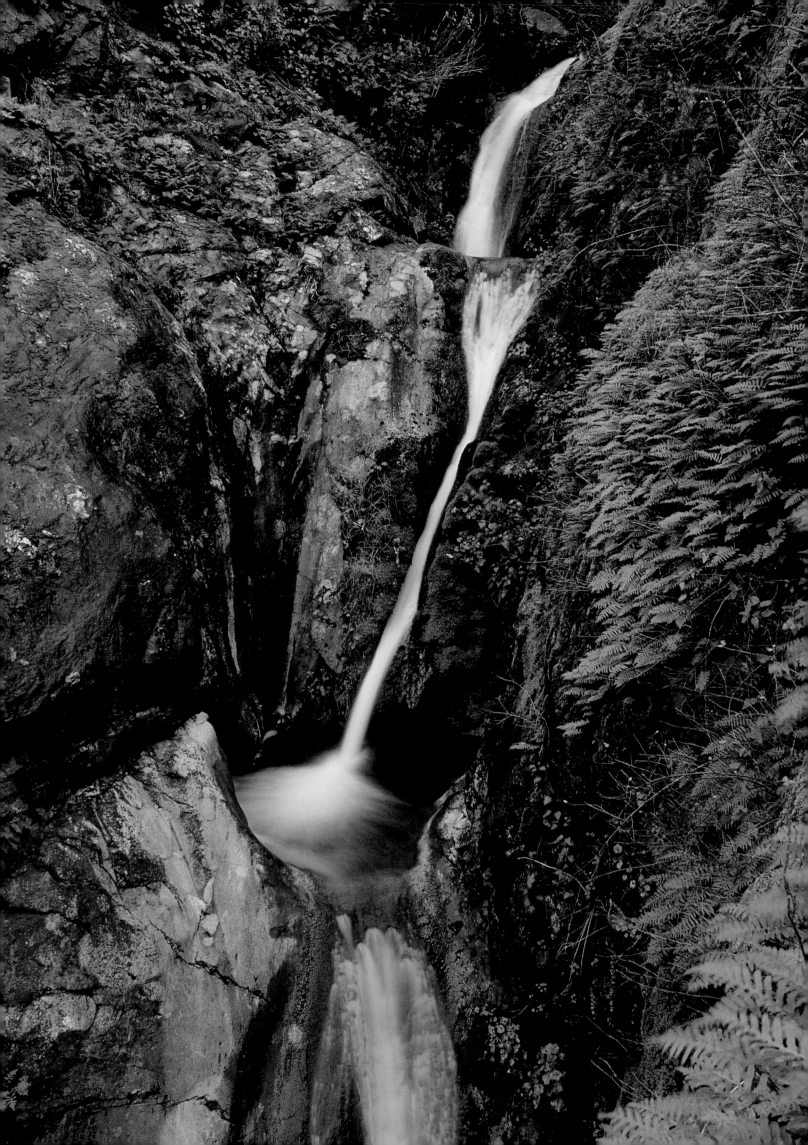

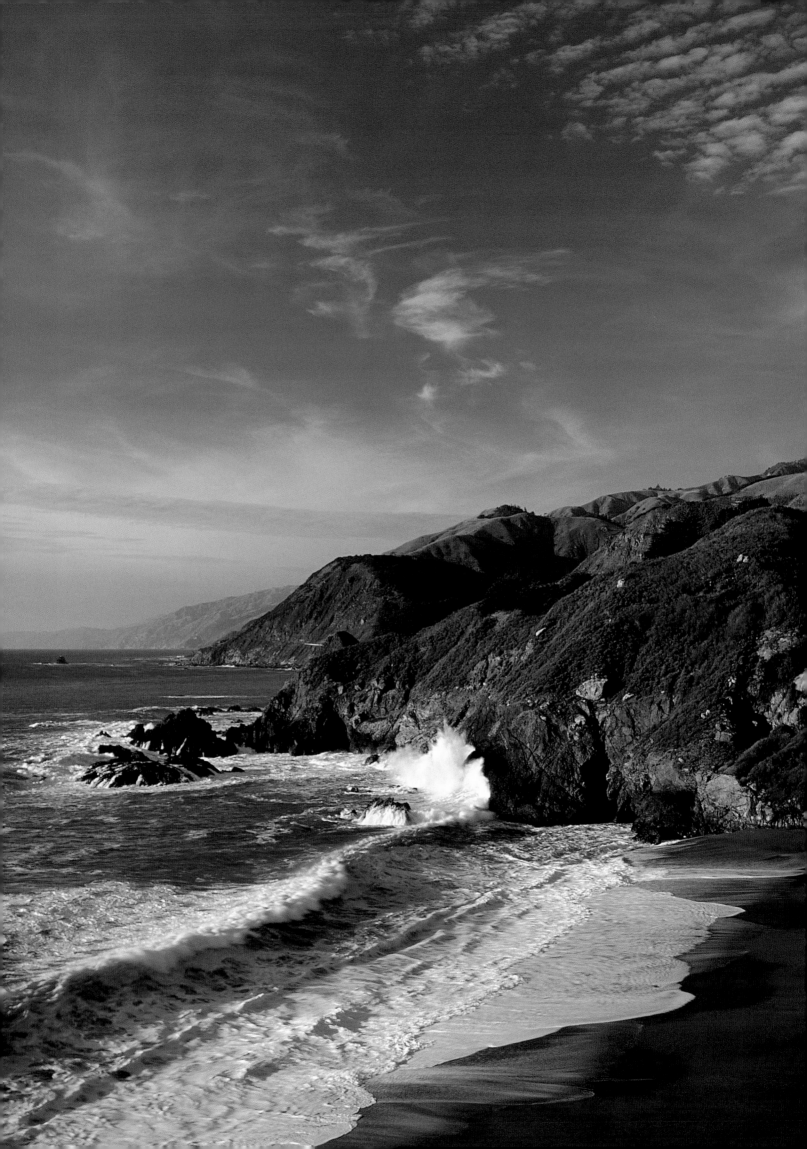

Explorations

I HAVE TO STOP AND LOOK. The wind is a vital force blowing across the fields in gusts. The grass bends in tall green waves as if some large hand were stroking it. The rhythm is captivating. Then I look behind me to the other side of the highway where the cobalt blue ocean surges and crashes into the rocks below, and I know this is one of those special moments that will be etched in my memory for years to come.

Many of us recall our first visit to the Big Sur Coast. The stunning views almost force you to pull to the side of the road and take more time to explore the rocky shoreline. On a foggy day the mists obscure the horizon, adding mystery and depth to this ever-changing panorama. On a clear day, when the grass is green and the sky and the Pacific Ocean are blue, there are numerous cars parked at the many vista points where visitors and locals alike can experience the extraordinary and relatively unpopulated stretches of coastline.

It was a propitious moment when The Big Sur Land Trust and I decided to publish a book featuring their properties. The Land Trust is a remarkable organization with a clearly defined and valuable mission: to preserve for future generations as much of the Big Sur coastline and other pristine areas of the Monterey Peninsula as possible. I was looking for a way to support these efforts, and the thought of exploring and capturing the beauty of this spectacular place on film offered a unique and challenging opportunity. We worked from the premise that sharing images of these areas with a wide audience would increase awareness of the breadth and natural beauty of the Monterey Peninsula and that this exposure would contribute to the success and ongoing efforts of The Land Trust.

We all have conversations about changes we see in places we love, how our favorite spots have become overpopulated and overdeveloped. Now, at least we know that vast, sweeping areas of the Big Sur coastline, from Monterey south to San Simeon, are protected from development. Thanks in large part to The Big Sur Land Trust, visitors today enjoy the same rhythmic patterns of wind and waves that are still fresh in my mind from my first visit to this dramatic shoreline more than thirty years ago.

—Douglas Steakley

Left: Breaking surf at Gamboa Beach.

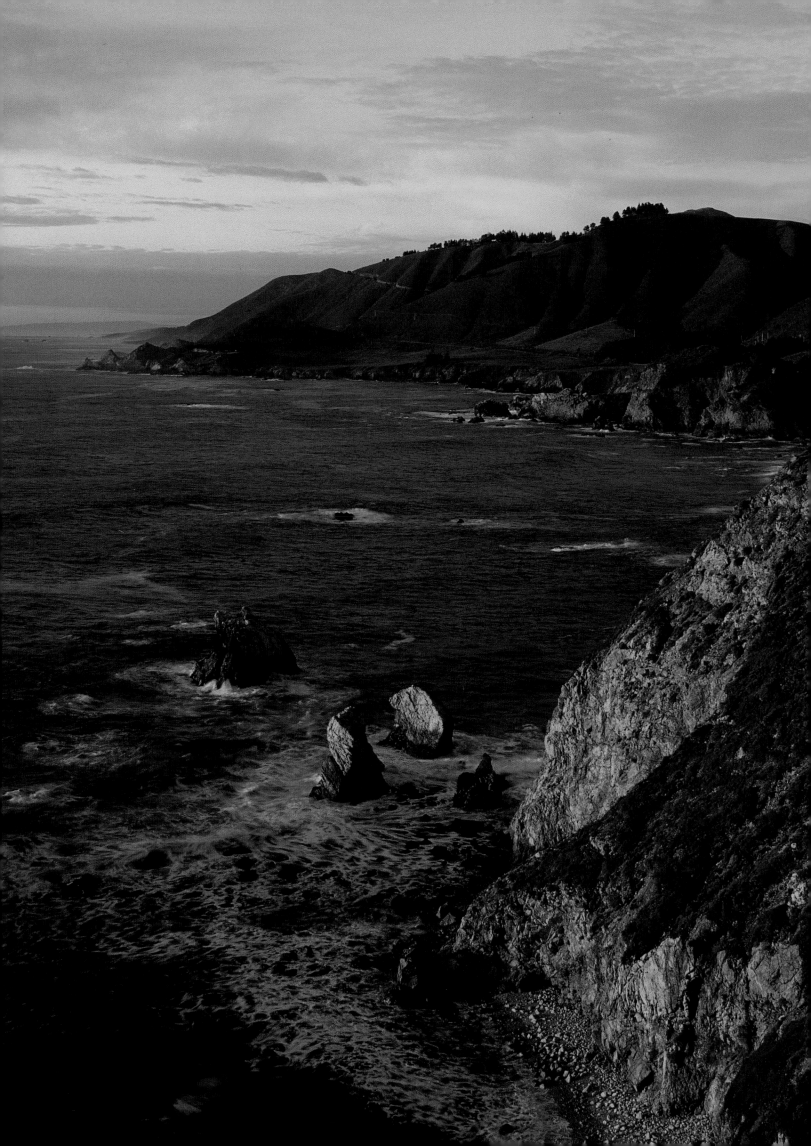

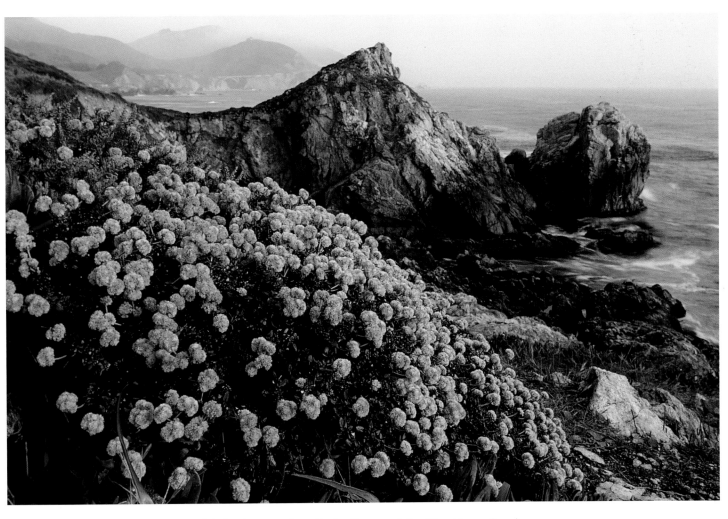

Left: Looking north to Rocky Point and the Glen Deven Ranch.
Above: Colorful buckwheat decorating the Rocky Point area.

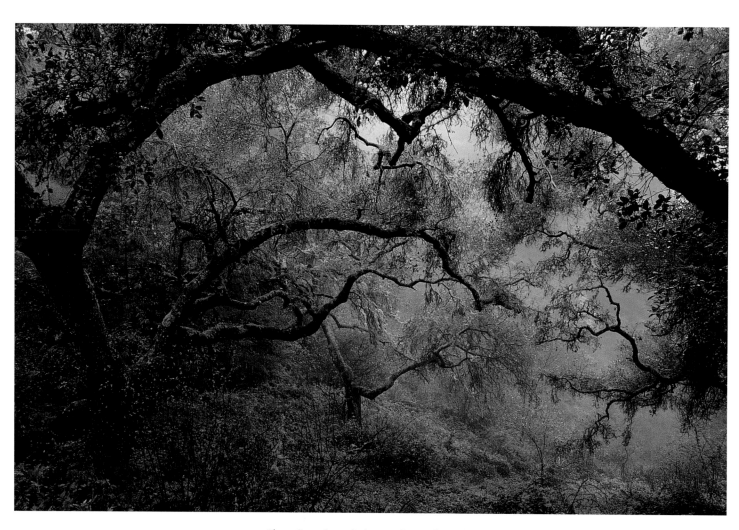

Above: Fog-shrouded coast live oaks in Big Sur.
Right: Waterfalls along Williams Creek in the Mitteldorf Preserve.
Overleaf: Spring lupines in Mitteldorf Preserve.

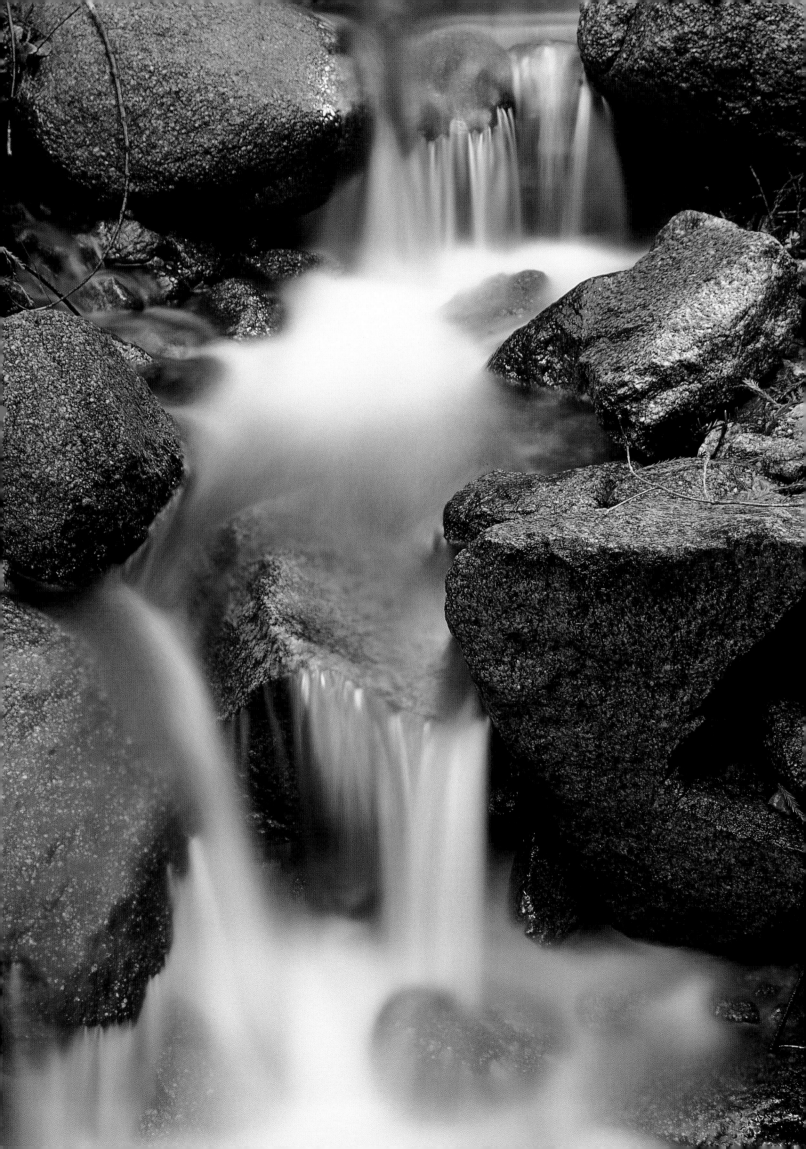

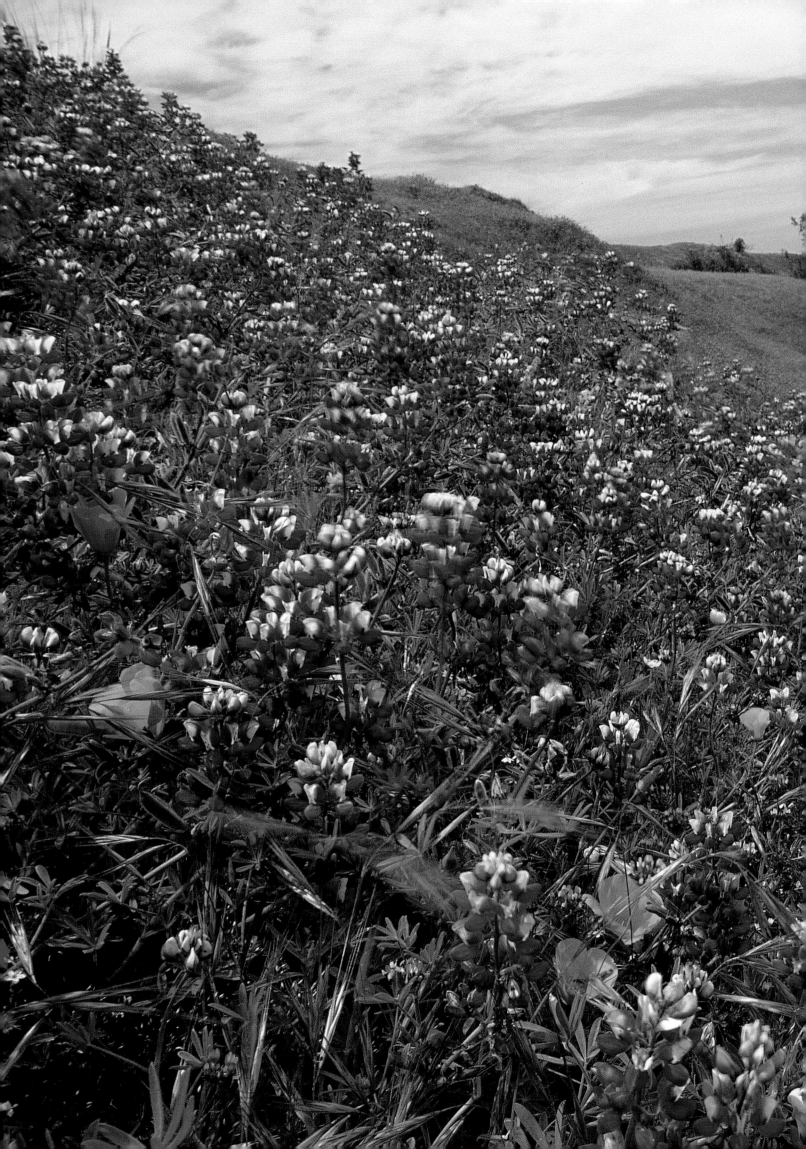

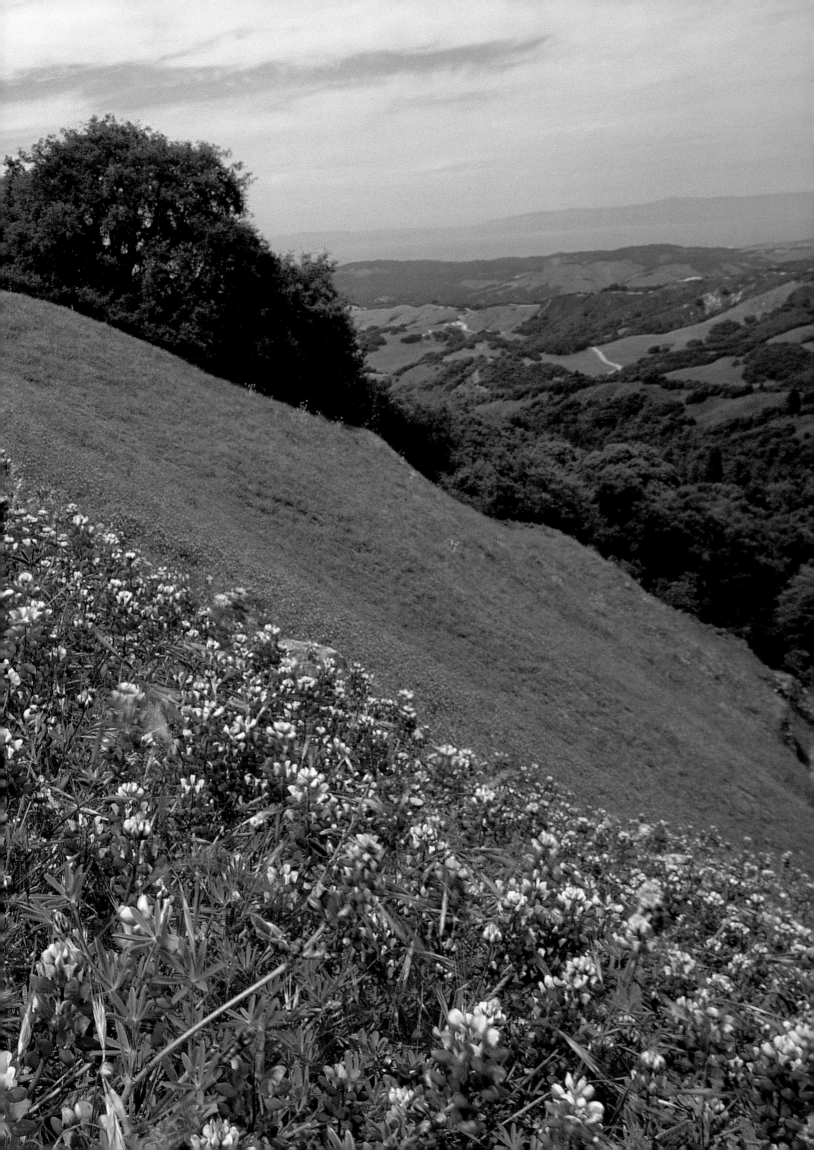

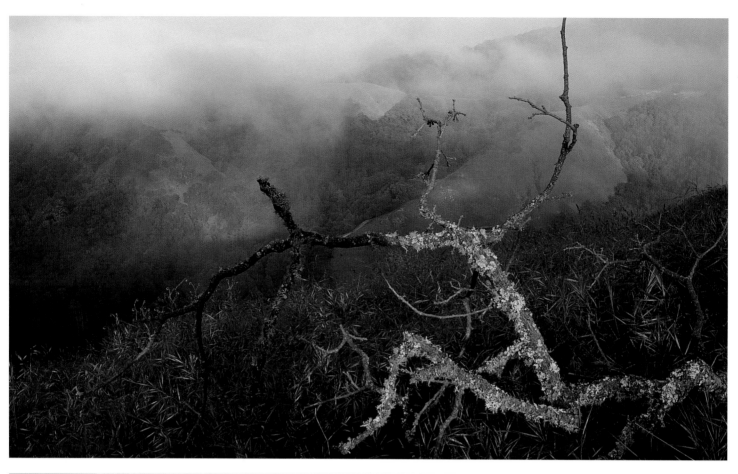

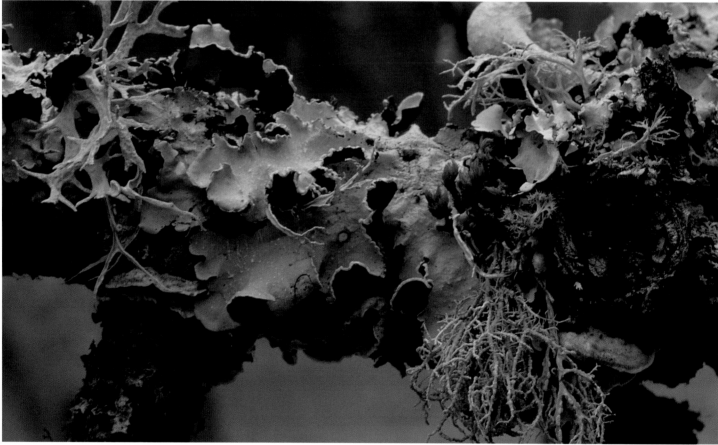

Above top: Evening fog over Echo Ridge at Mitteldorf Preserve.
Above bottom: Lichen-covered branch at Garland Ranch Regional Park expansion.

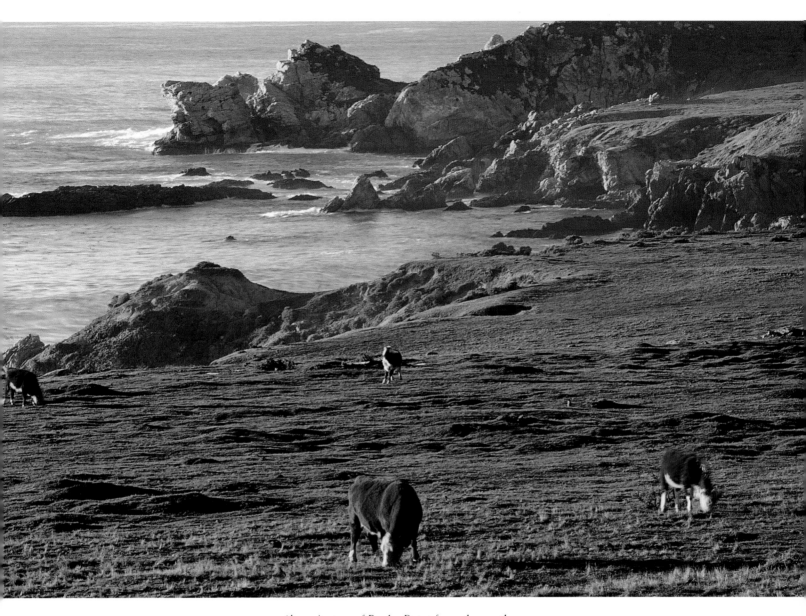

Above: A view of Rocky Point from the south.
Overleaf: A clash of land and sea at Hurricane Point, Bixby Ocean Ranch.

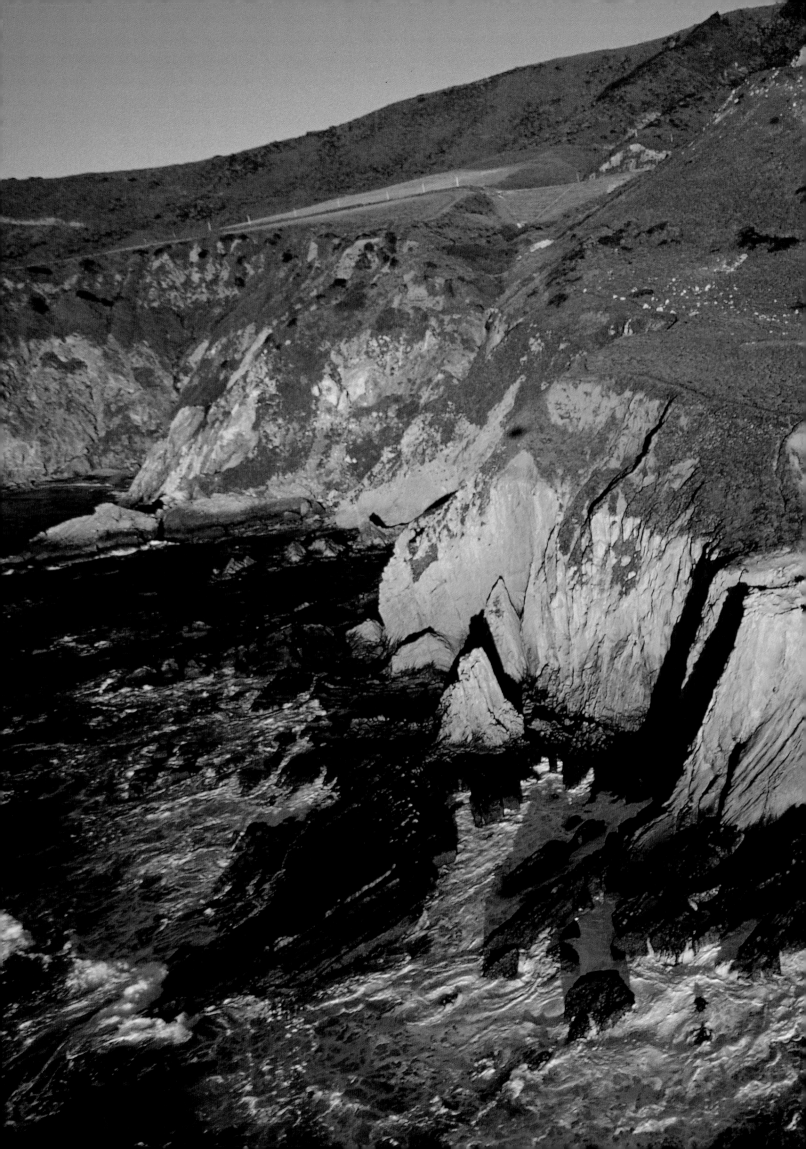

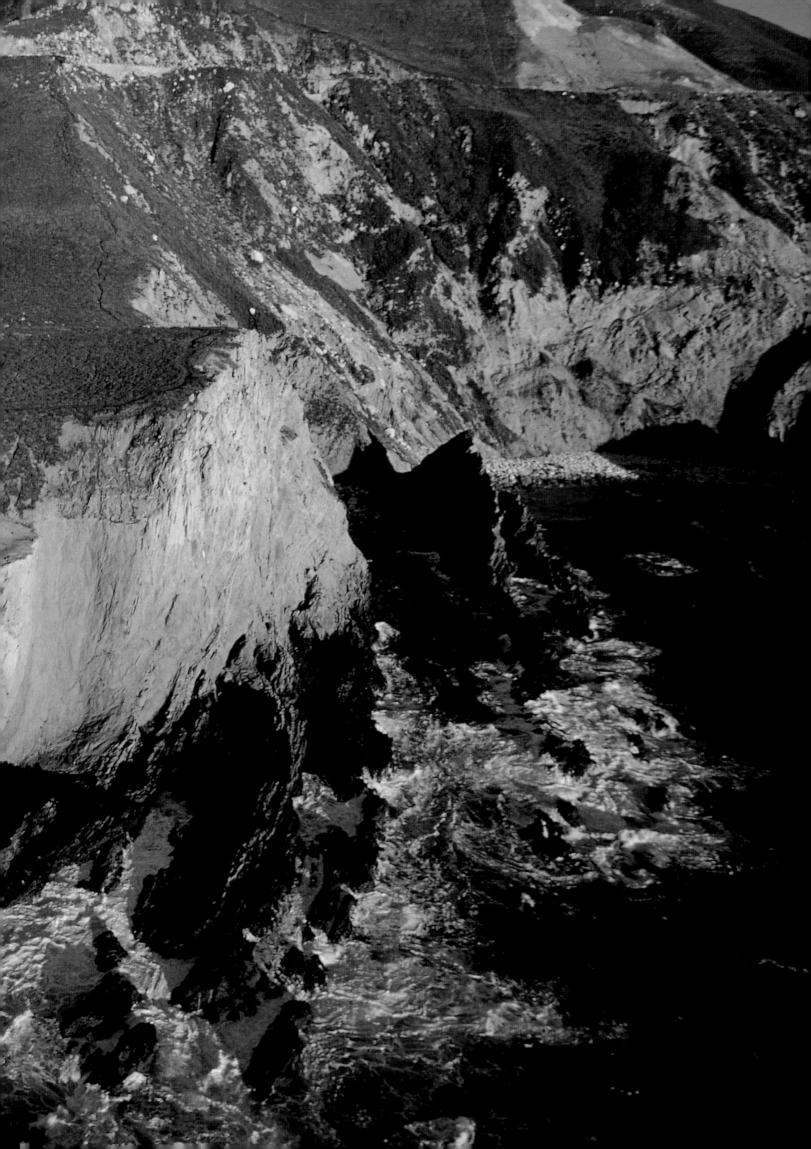

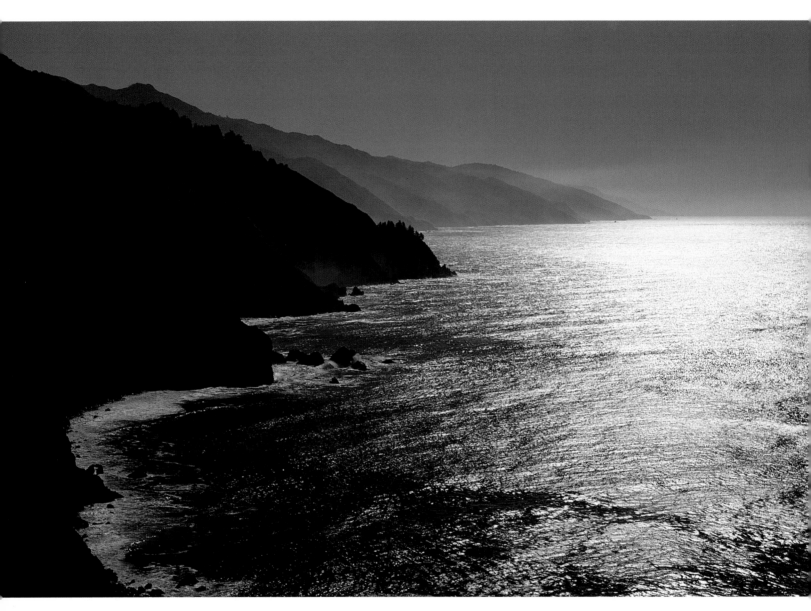

Above: View south along the Big Sur coastline.

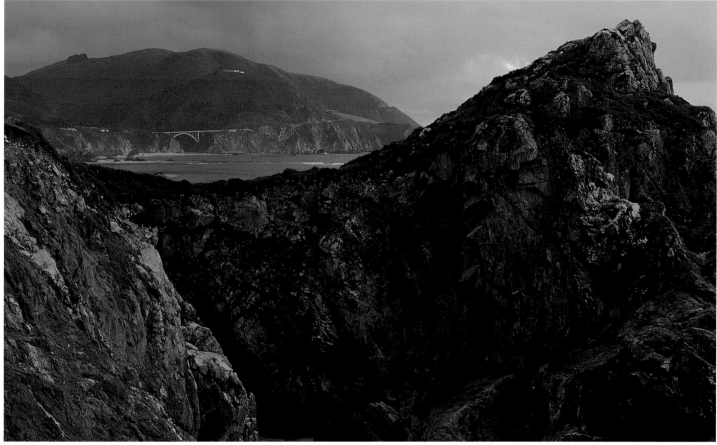

Above top: Monterey pine silhouette, Point Lobos Ranch.
Above bottom: Rocky Creek Bridge, as seen from Rocky Point.

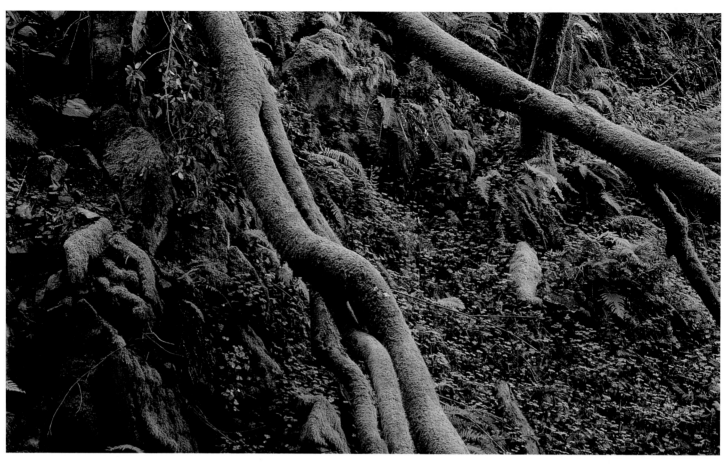

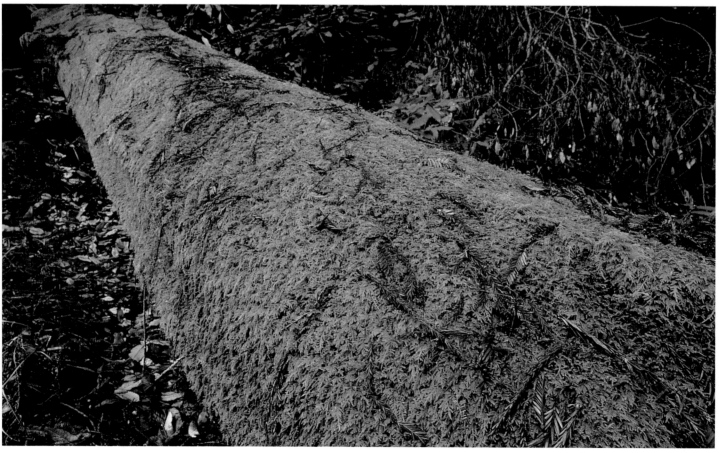

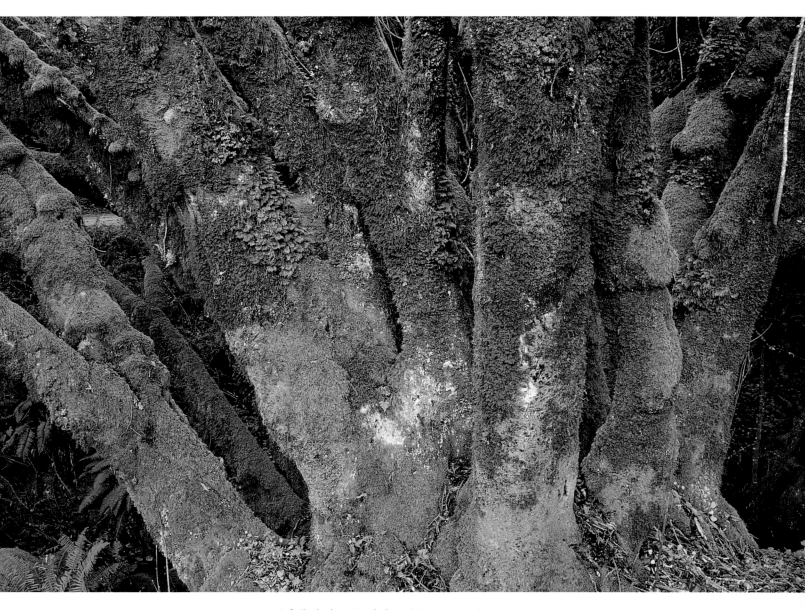

Left (both photos) and above: Moss-covered trees
along the Big Sur Coast and in the Mitteldorf Preserve.

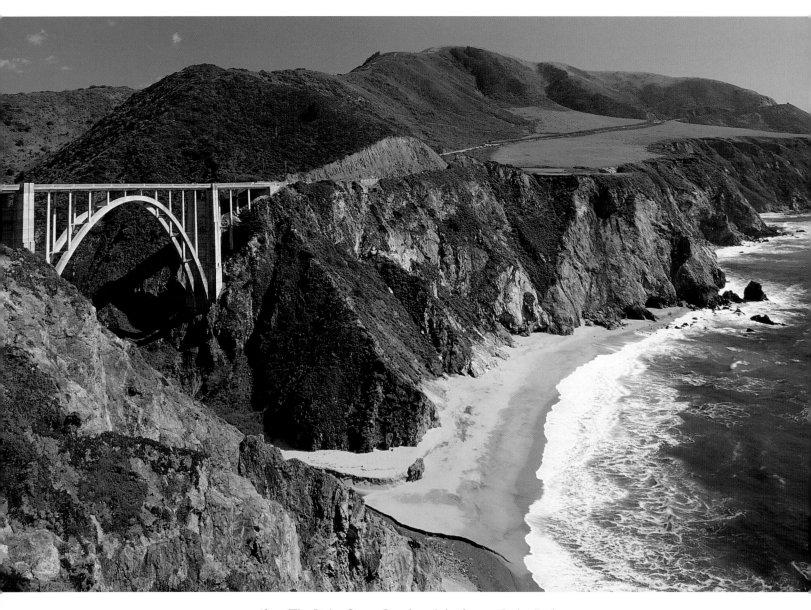

Above: The Bixby Ocean Ranch and the famous Bixby Bridge.

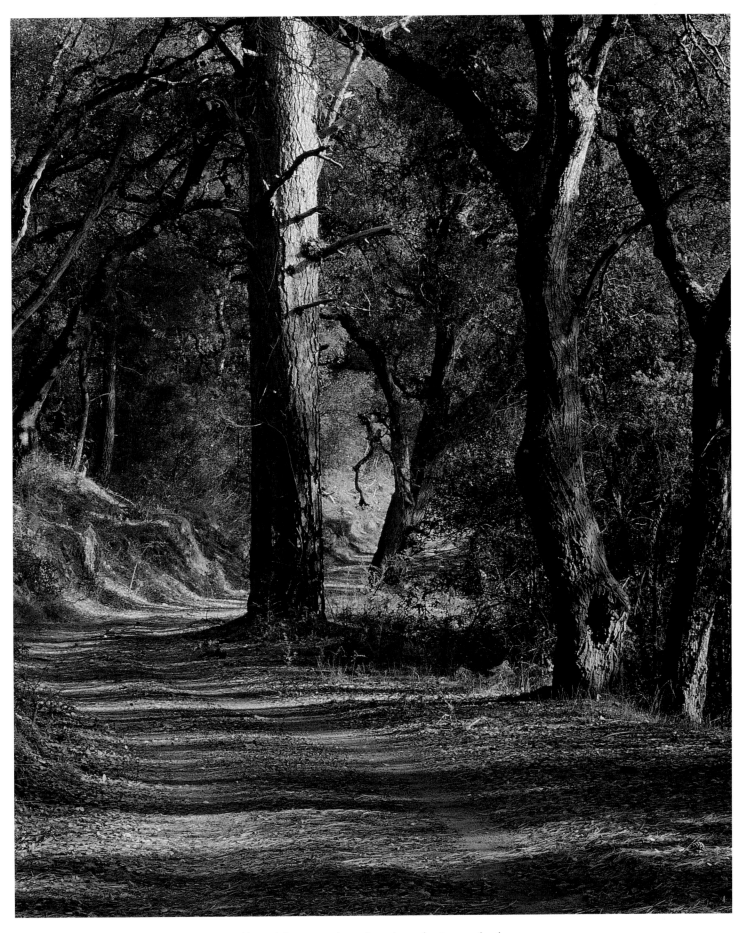

Above: A forest road winding through pines and oaks,
Big Sur south coast.

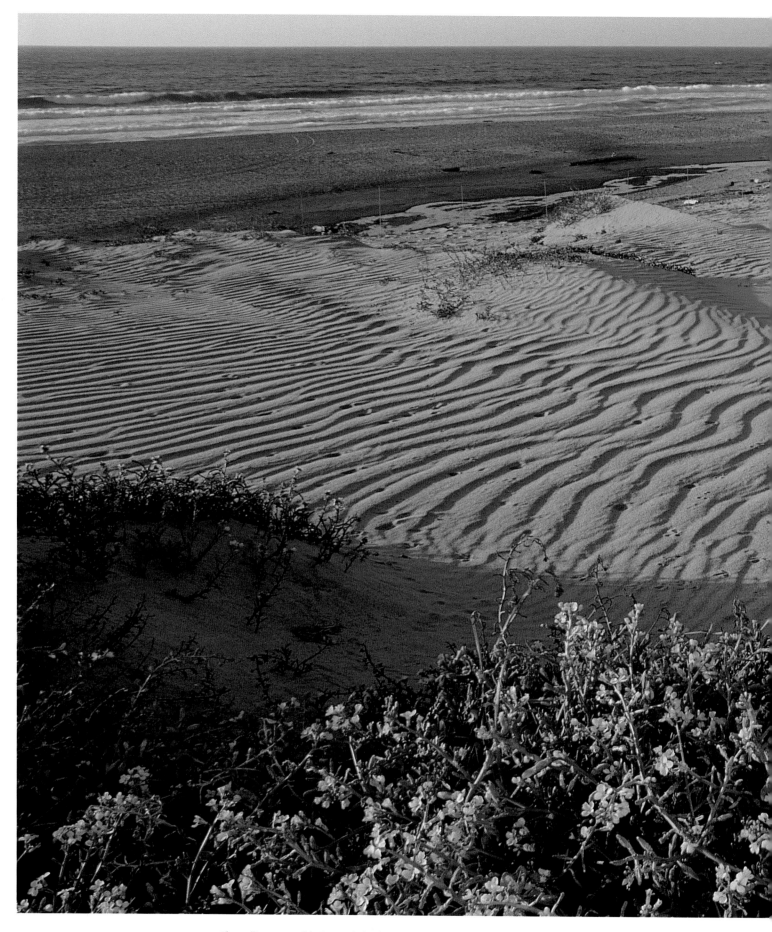

Above: Patterns of light and shadow on the Sand City Dunes,
Monterey Bay State Seashore.

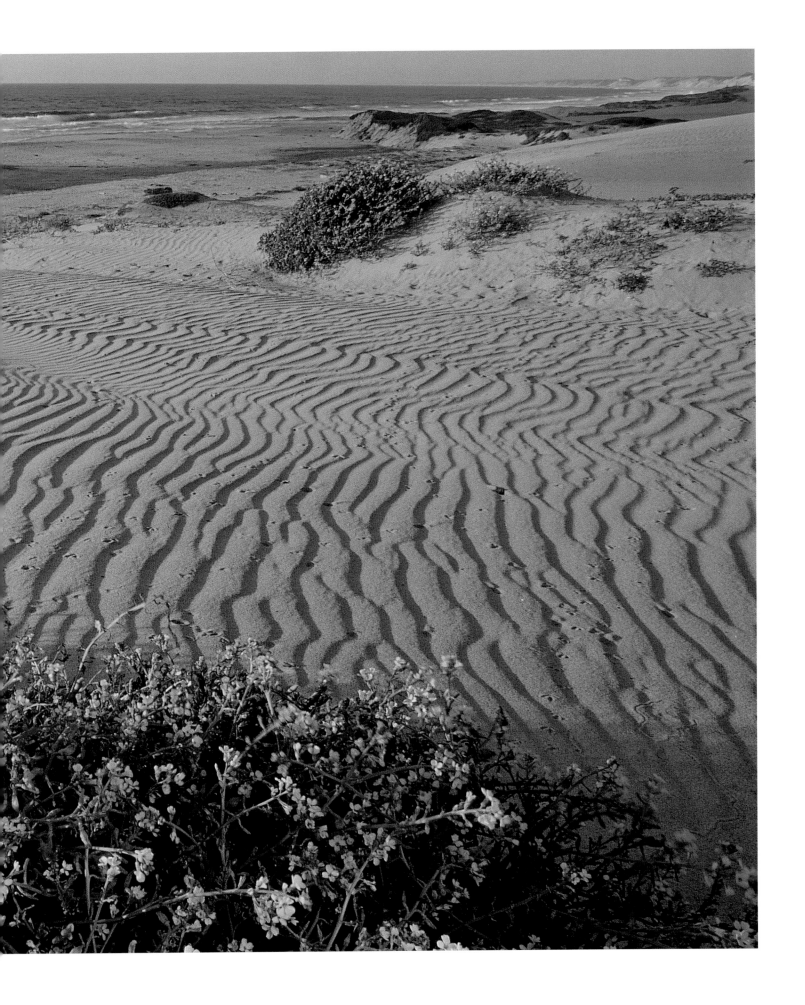

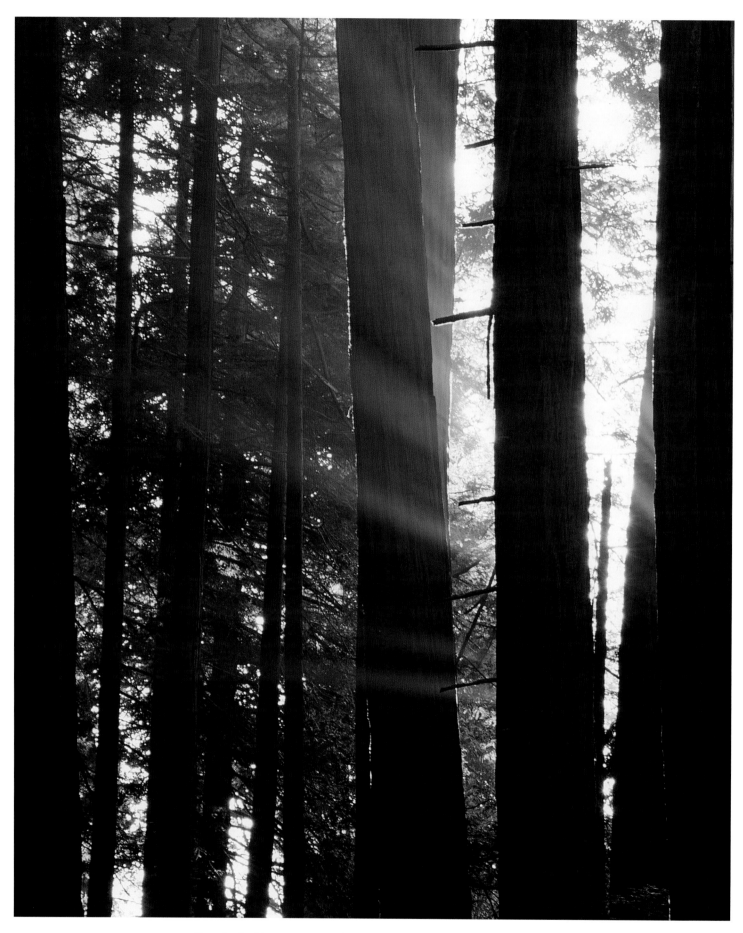

Above: Light filtering through the Mitteldorf Preserve's redwood forest.
Right: Moss in shaded redwood habitat at the Mitteldorf Preserve.
Overleaf: Plumes of spindrift off the surf near Carmel Point.

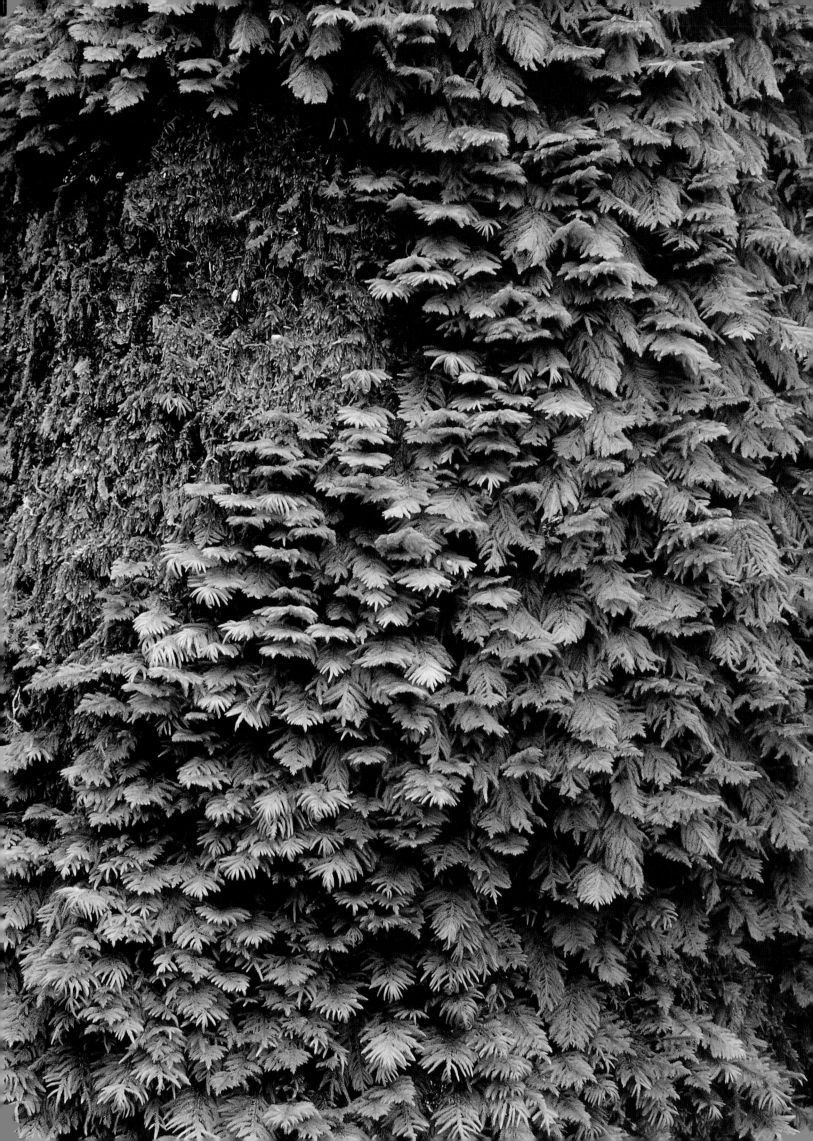

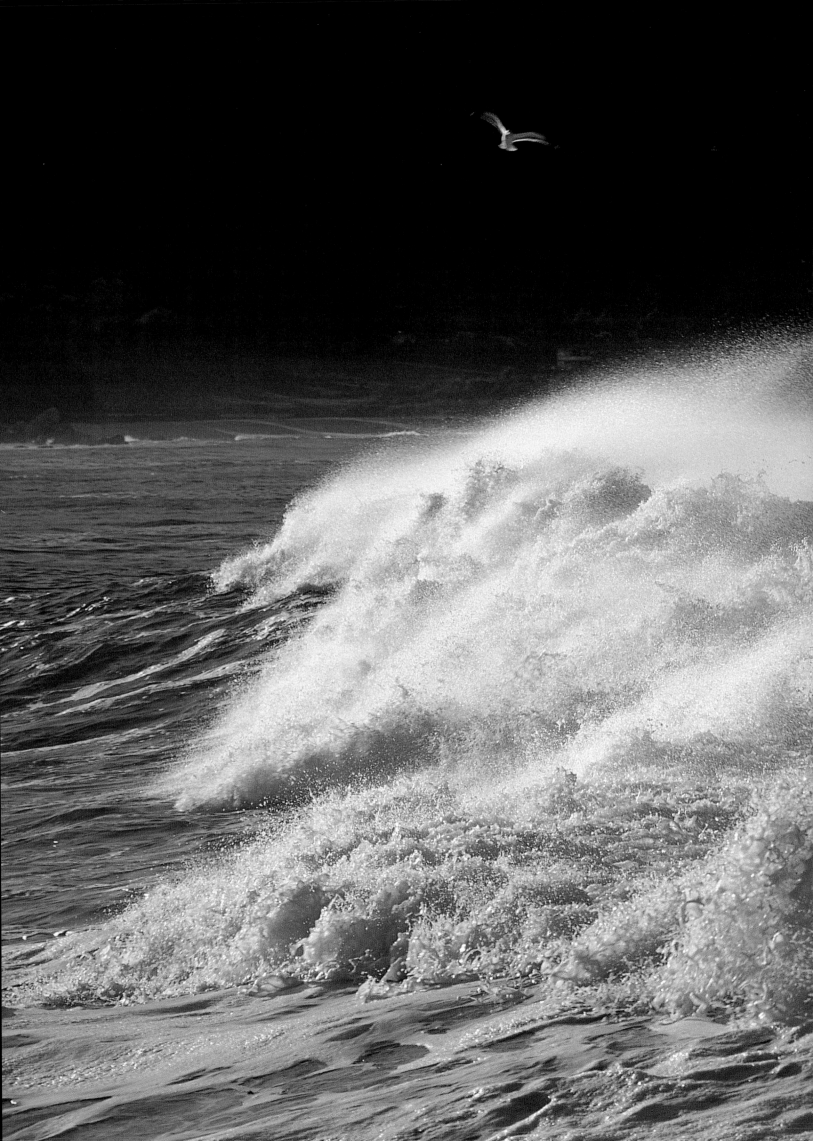

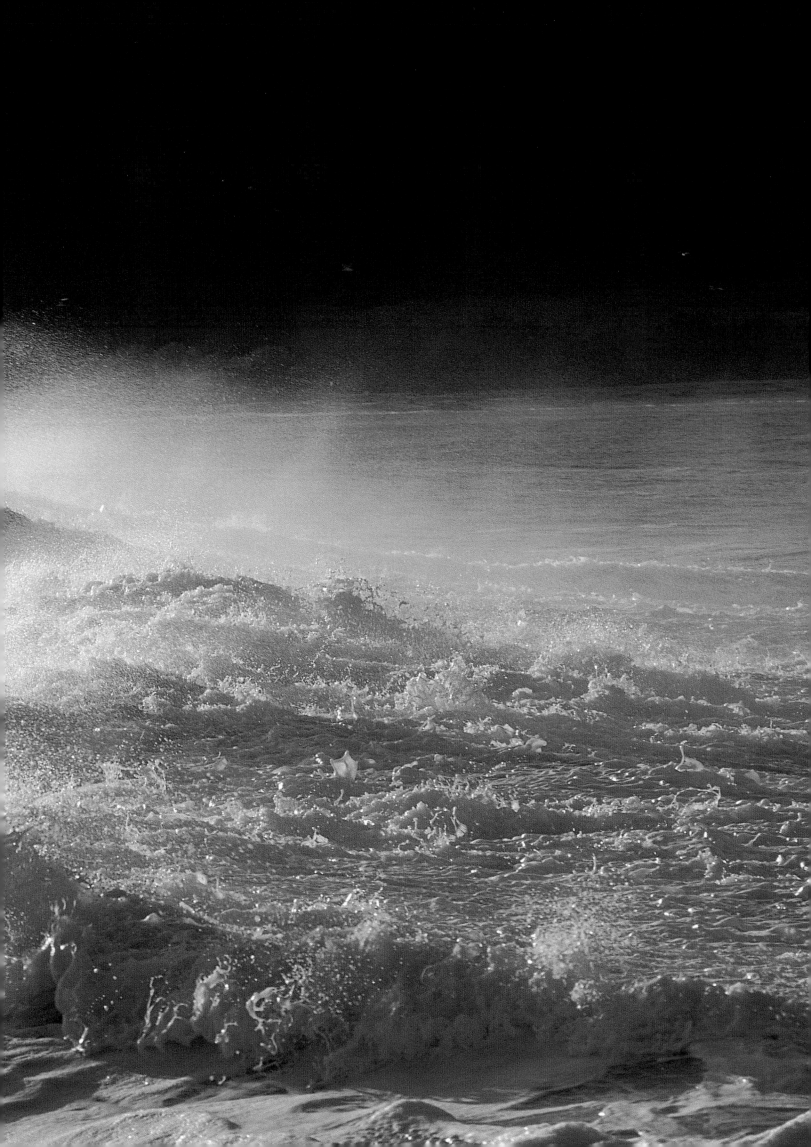

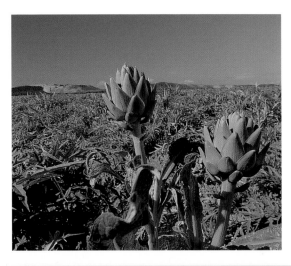

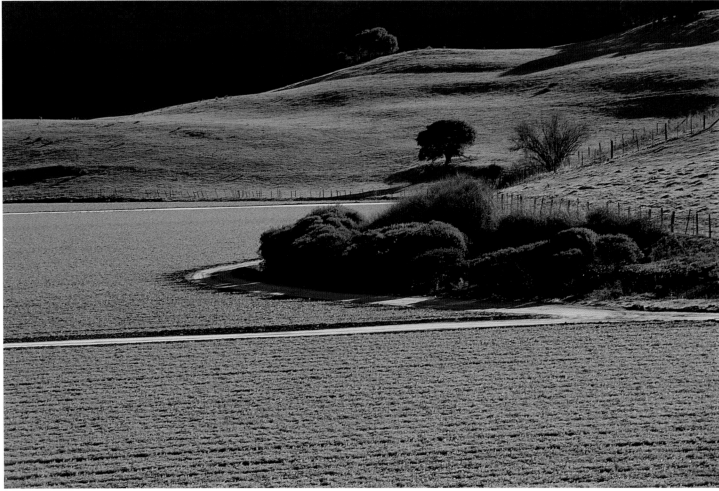

Above top: Artichokes near Martin Dunes.
Above bottom and right: Coast Ranch and the historic
Odello fields below the Palo Corona Ranch.
Overleaf: Highway 1 vista of the Little Sur
River estuary on the El Sur Ranch.

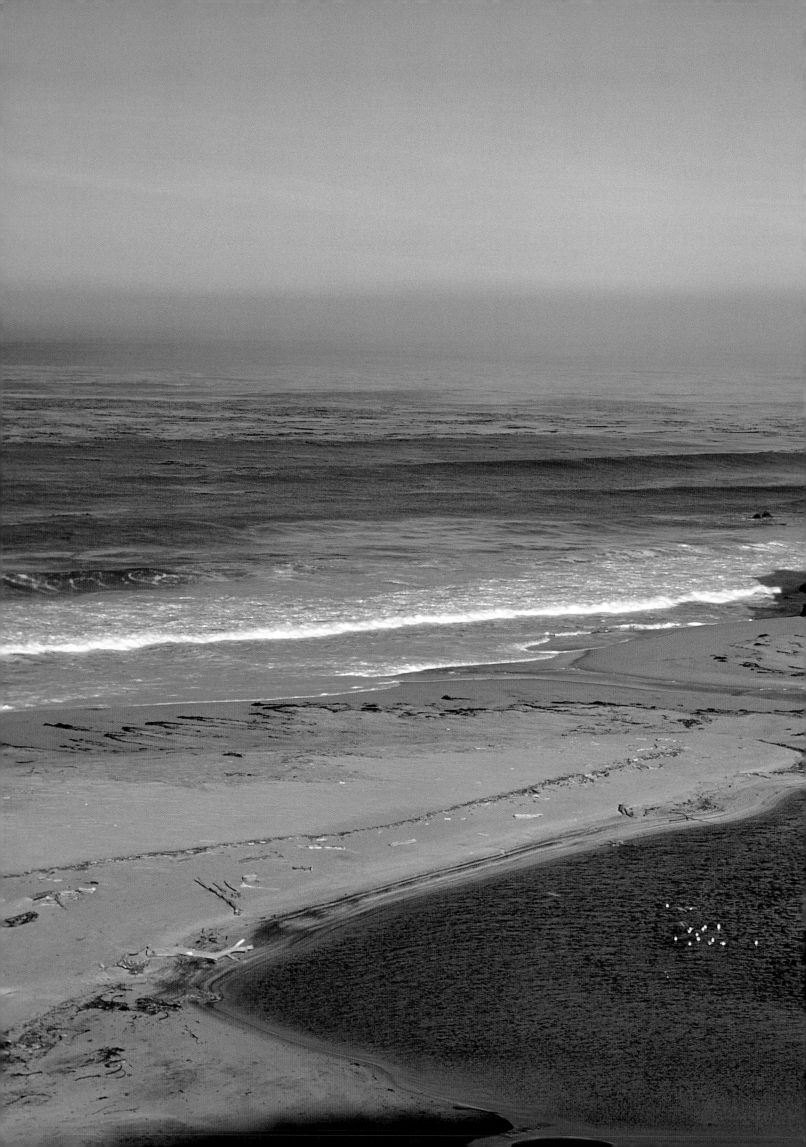

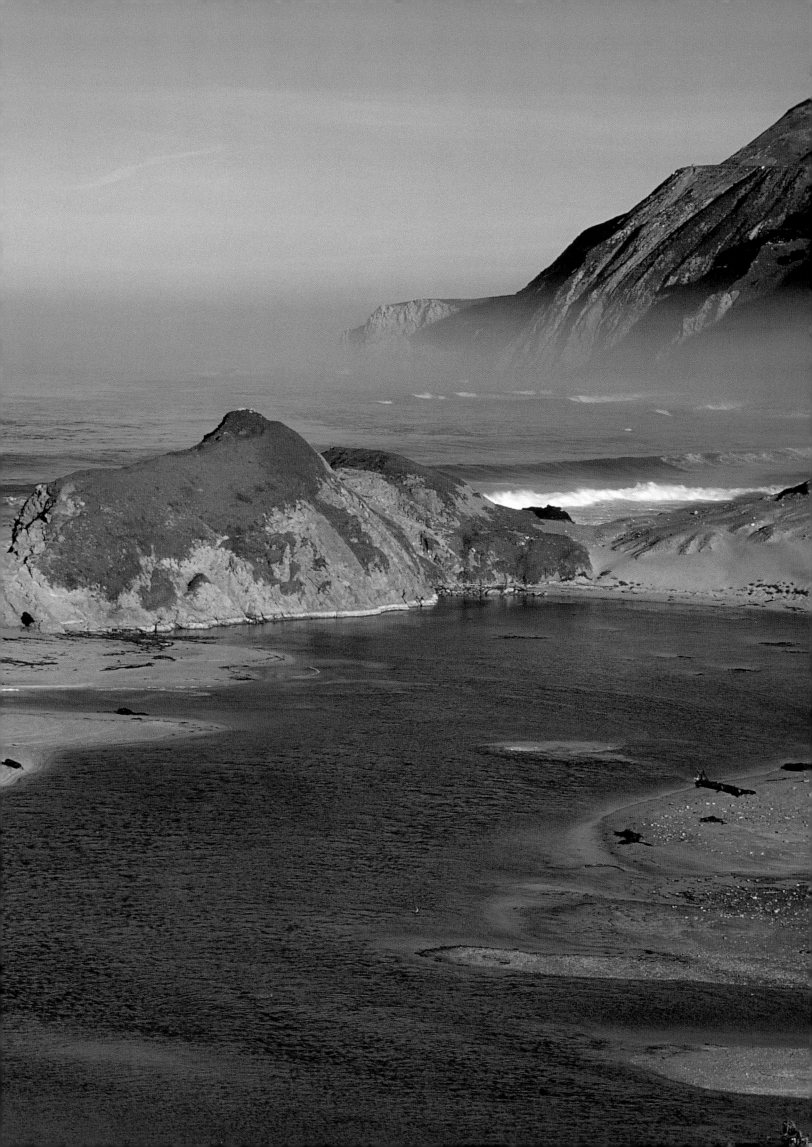

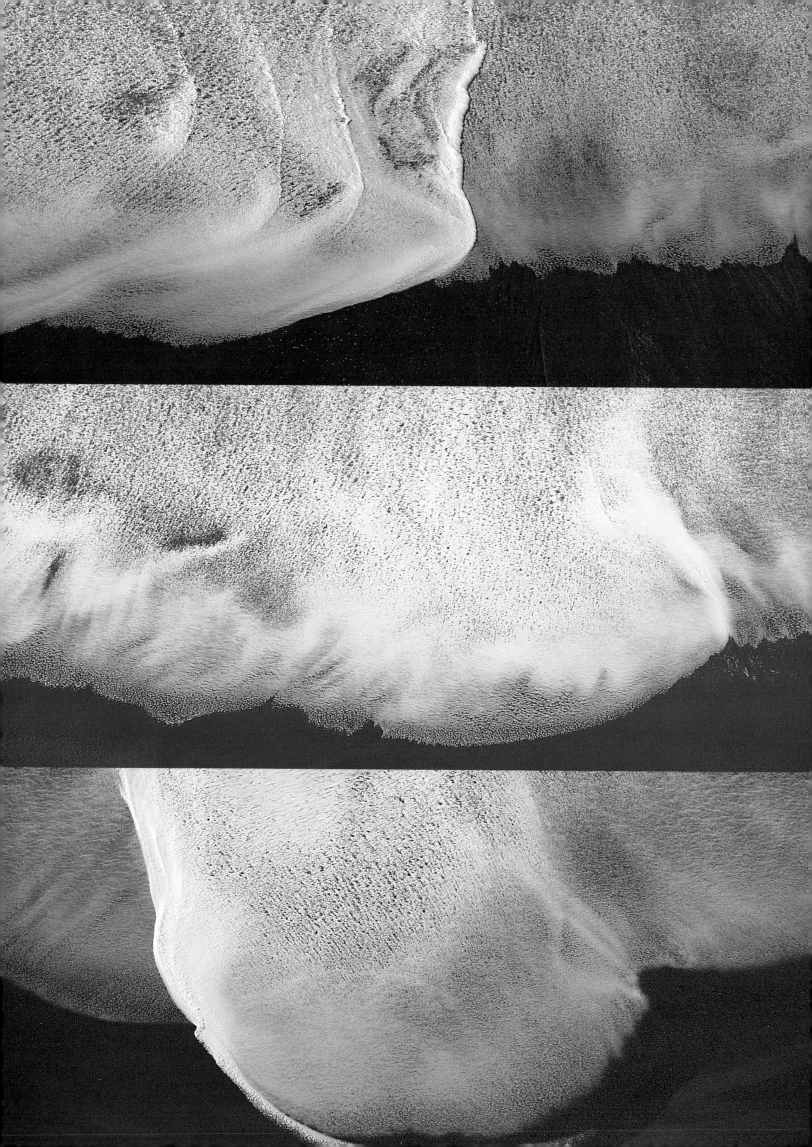

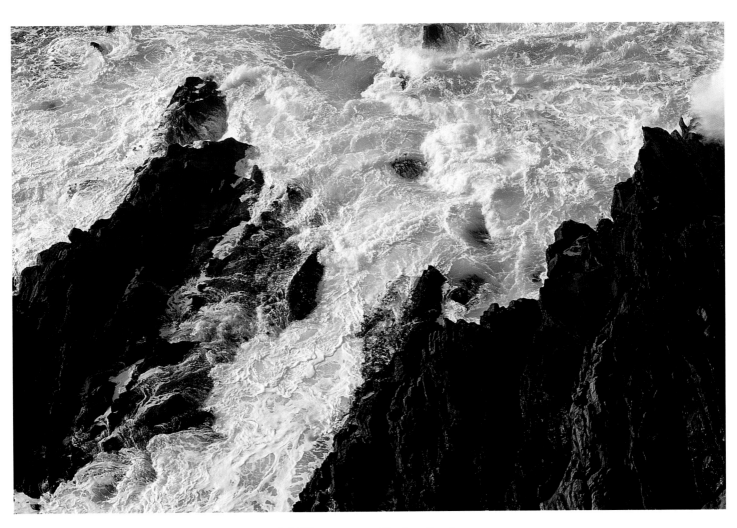

Left: Wave patterns, Gamboa Beach.
Above: High surf, Bixby Ocean Ranch.

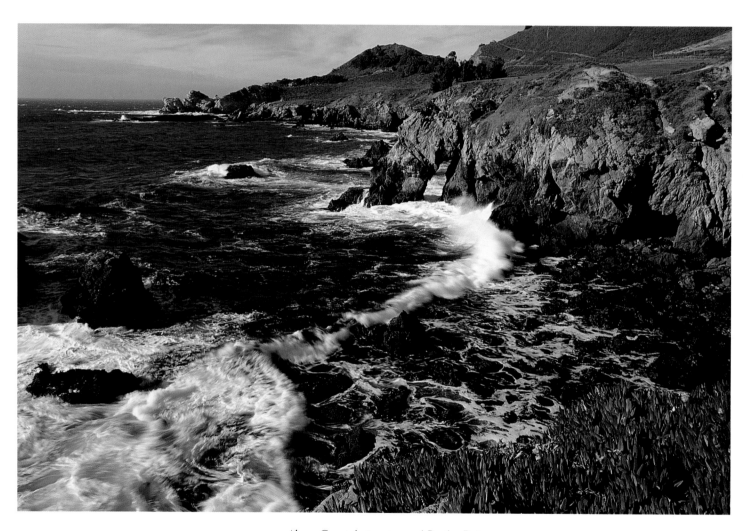

Above: Coastal view toward Rocky Point.

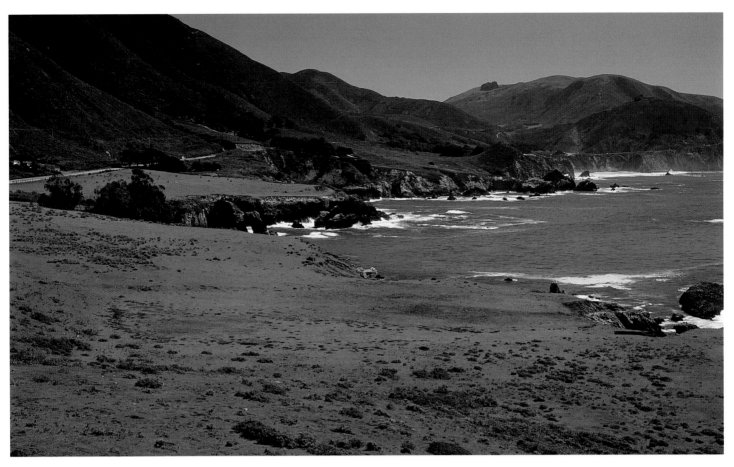

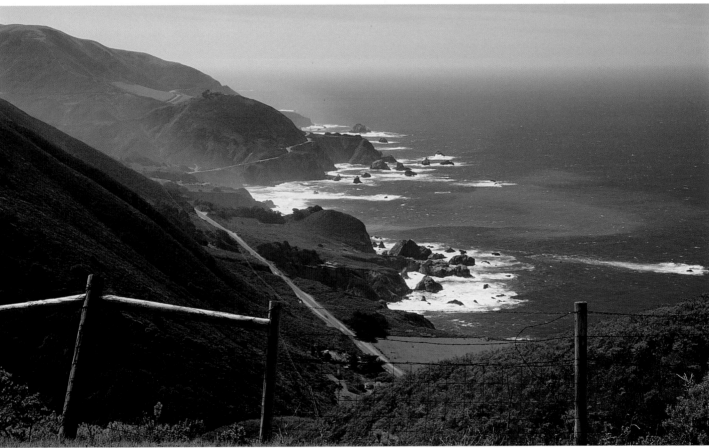

Above top: Historic Notley's Landing, as seen from Rocky Point.
Above bottom: Sweeping coastal views from the Glen Deven Ranch,
including Notley's Landing and the Bixby Ocean Ranch.

49

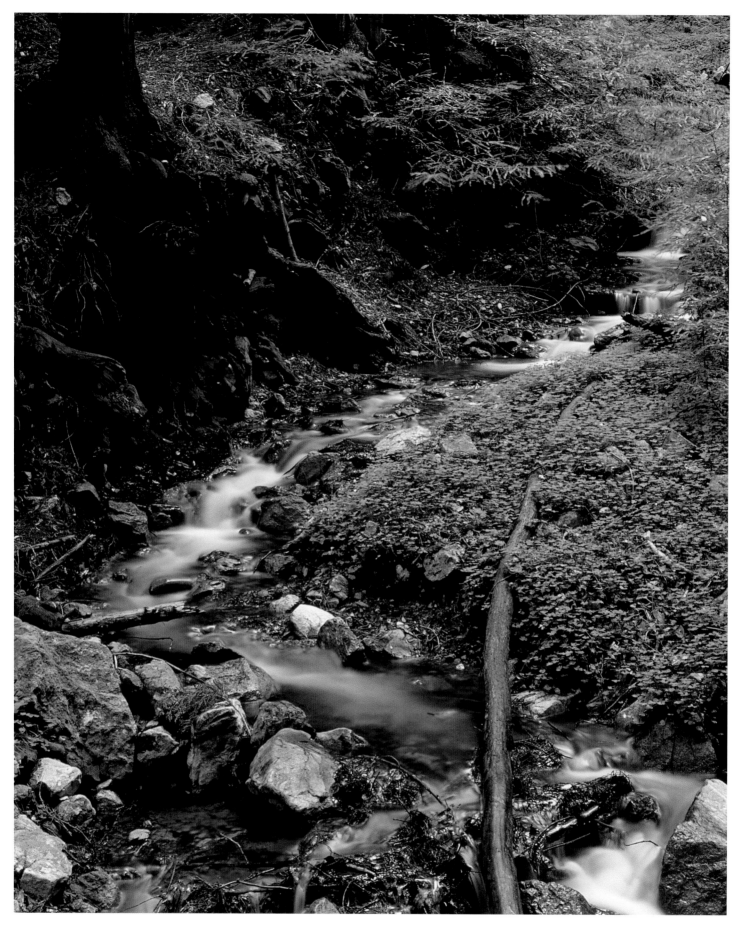

Above: Pheneger Creek, Esther Pfeiffer Ewoldsen addition
to the Los Padres National Forest.

50

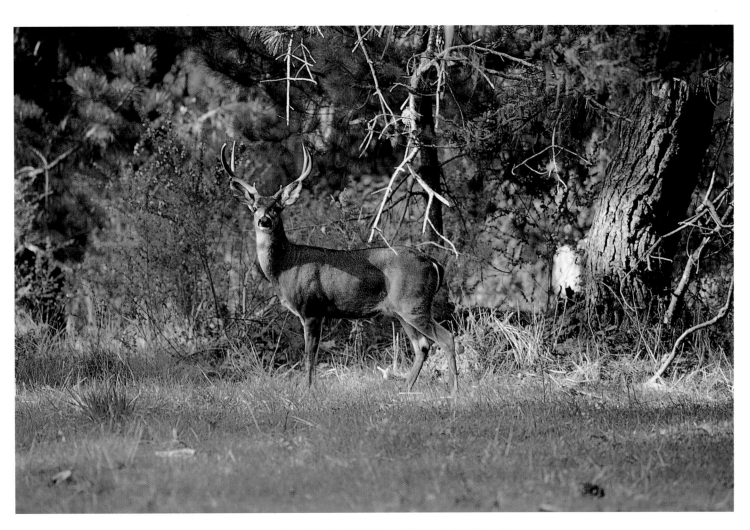

Above: Black-tailed deer at Point Lobos Ranch.

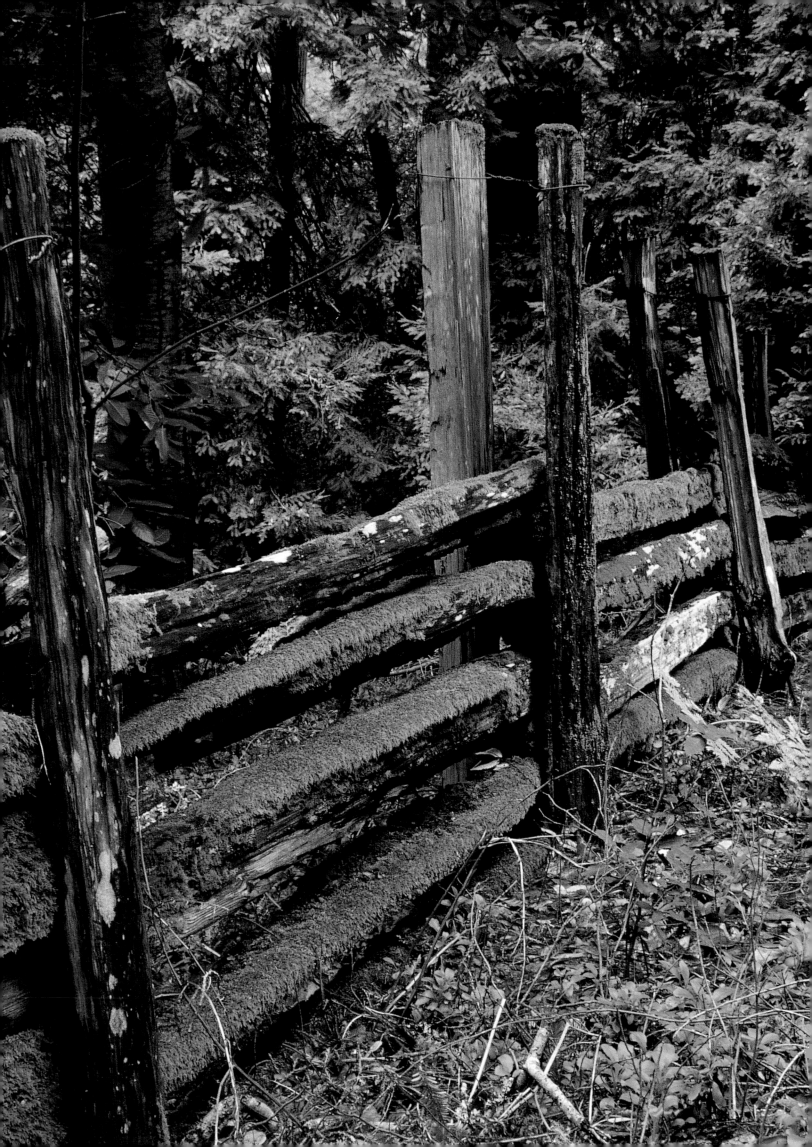

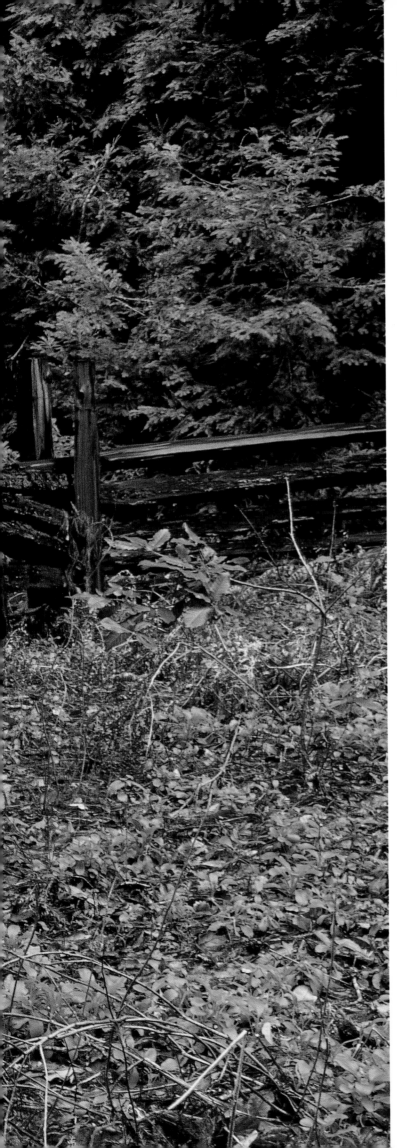

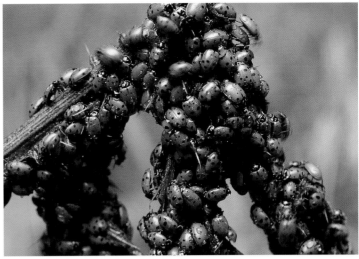

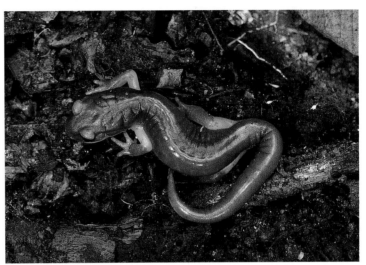

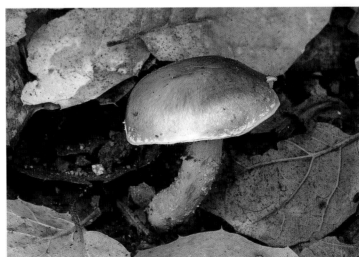

Left: Hand-split redwood fence at Mitteldorf Preserve.
Above top: Ladybugs hibernating at Mill Creek Preserve.
Above middle: Ensatina along Williams Creek
in the Mitteldorf Preserve.
Above bottom: Mushroom found in
Garland Ranch Regional Park expansion.

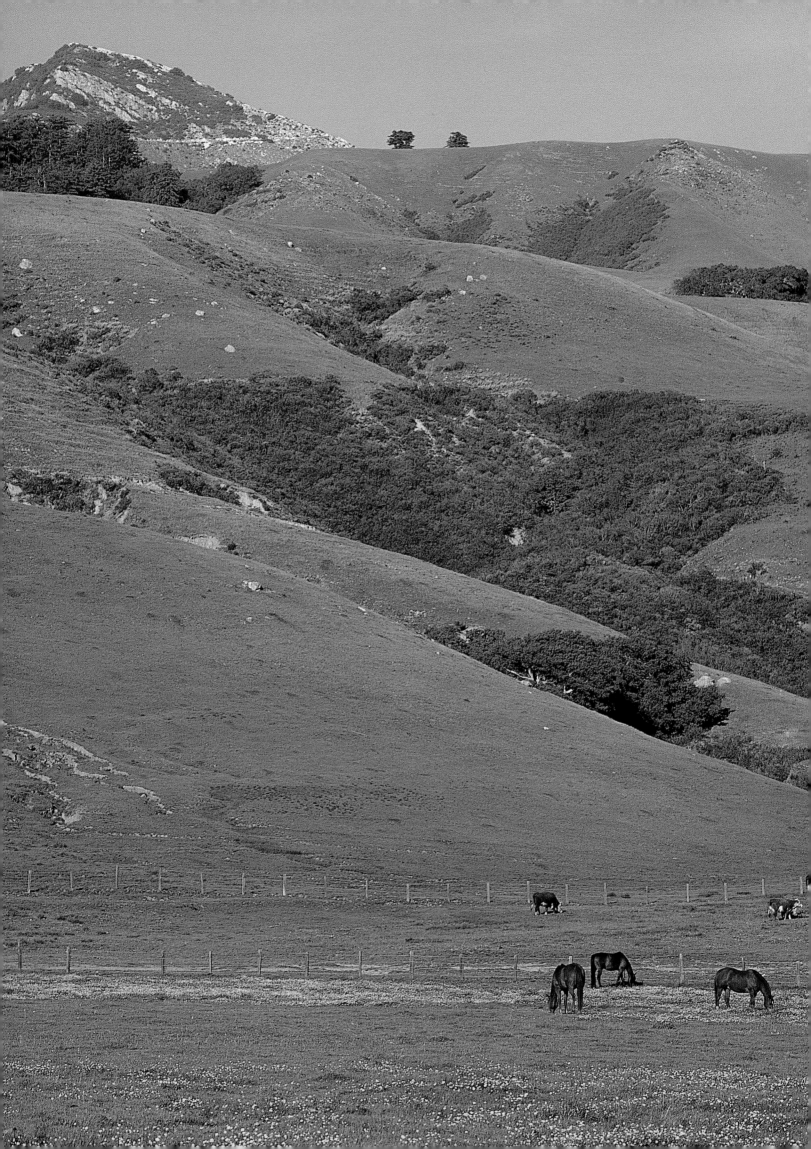

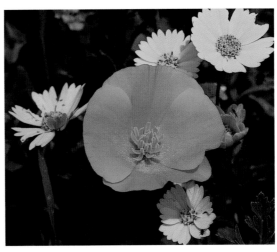

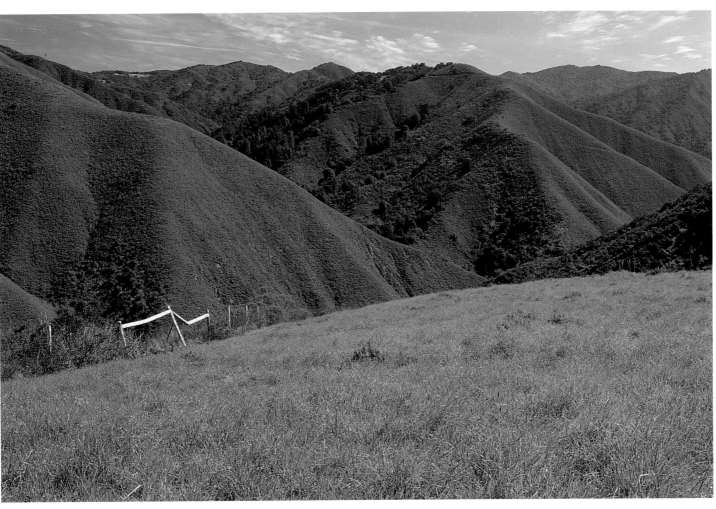

Left: Springtime at the El Sur Ranch and Pico Blanco from Highway 1.
Above top: A California poppy surrounded by Madia blossoms.
Above bottom: The rugged hills of Glen Deven Ranch.
Overleaf: Evening colors at Rocky Point.

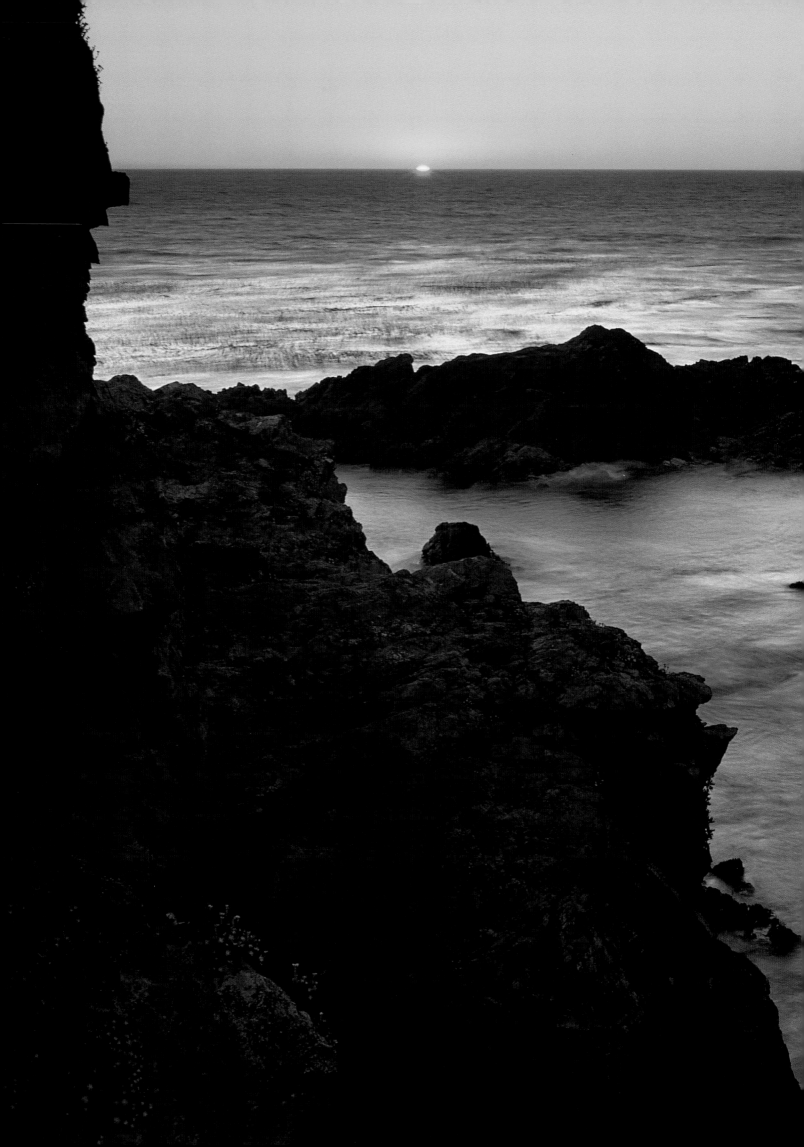

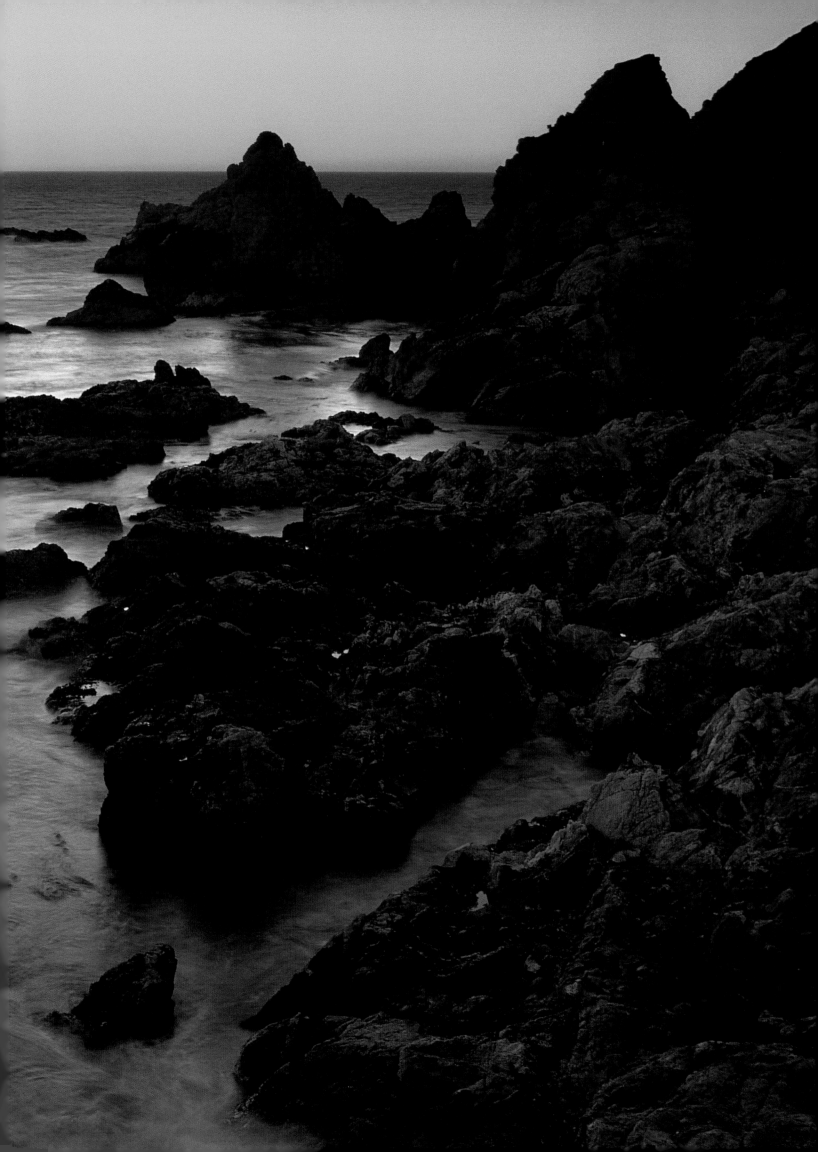

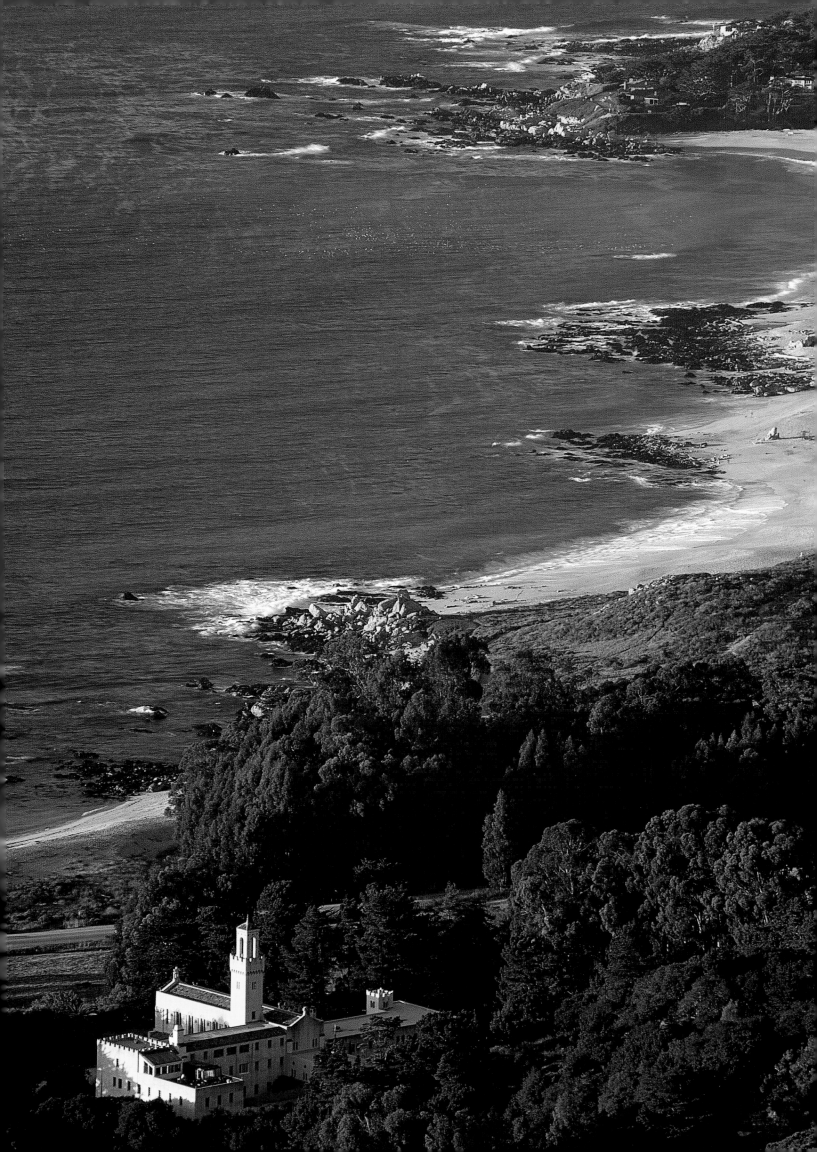

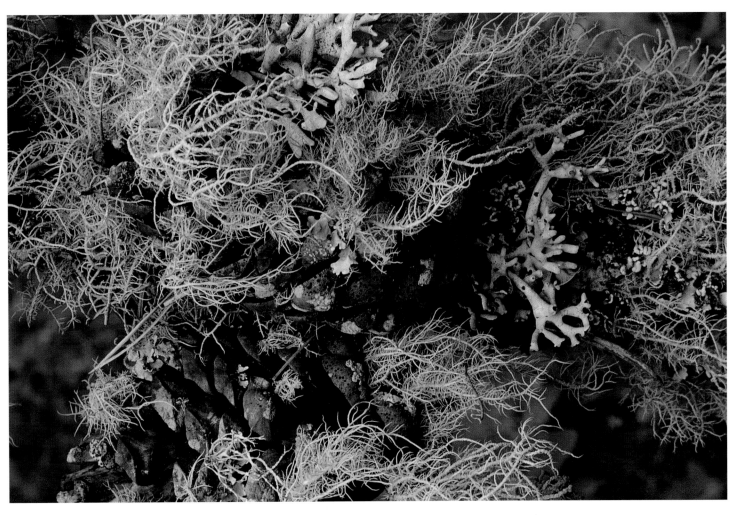

Left: Carmelite Monastery and
Carmel River State Beach from Point Lobos Ranch.
Above: Lichens and Monterey pine cones at Point Lobos Ranch.
Overleaf: A bird's-eye view of Highway 1 as it winds around
the mouth of the Little Sur River on El Sur Ranch.

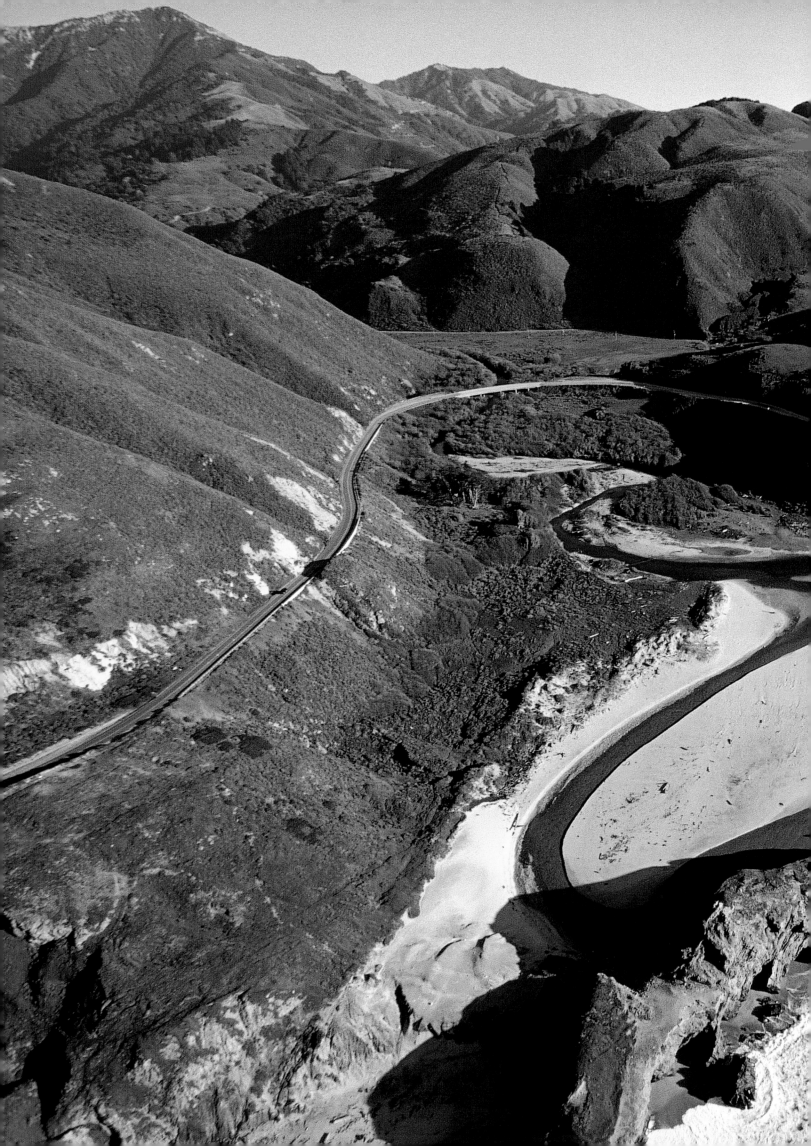

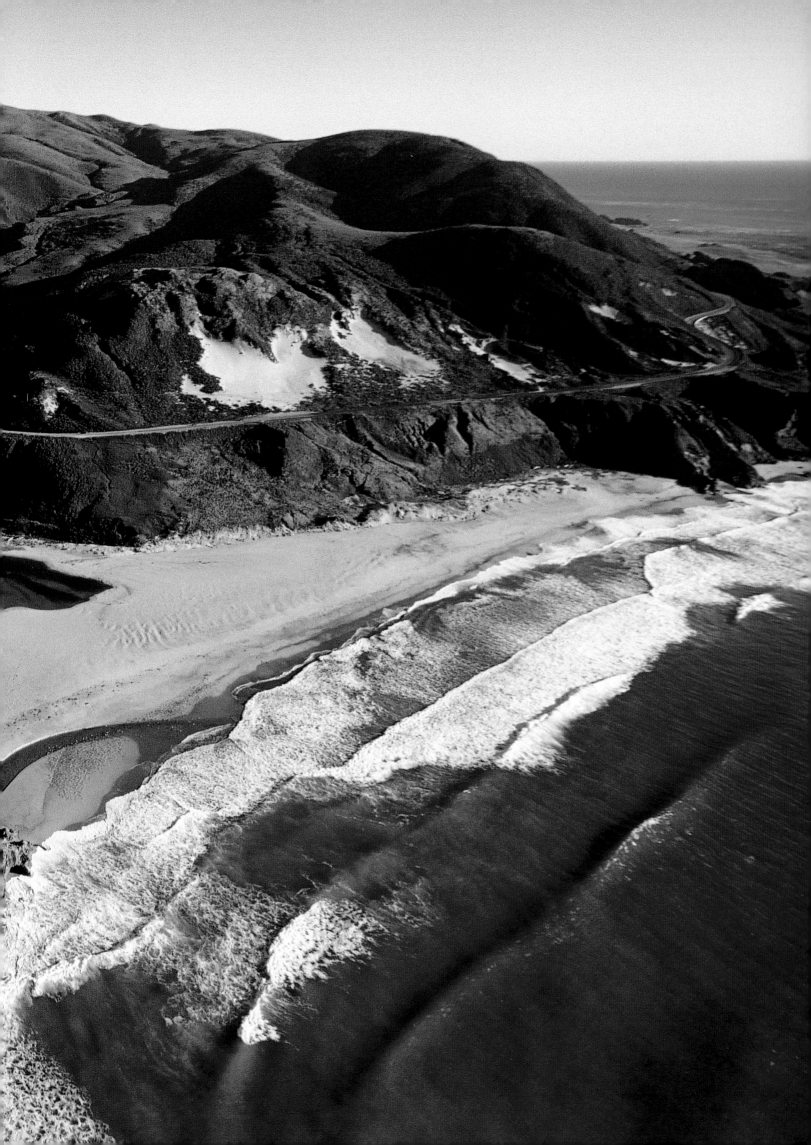

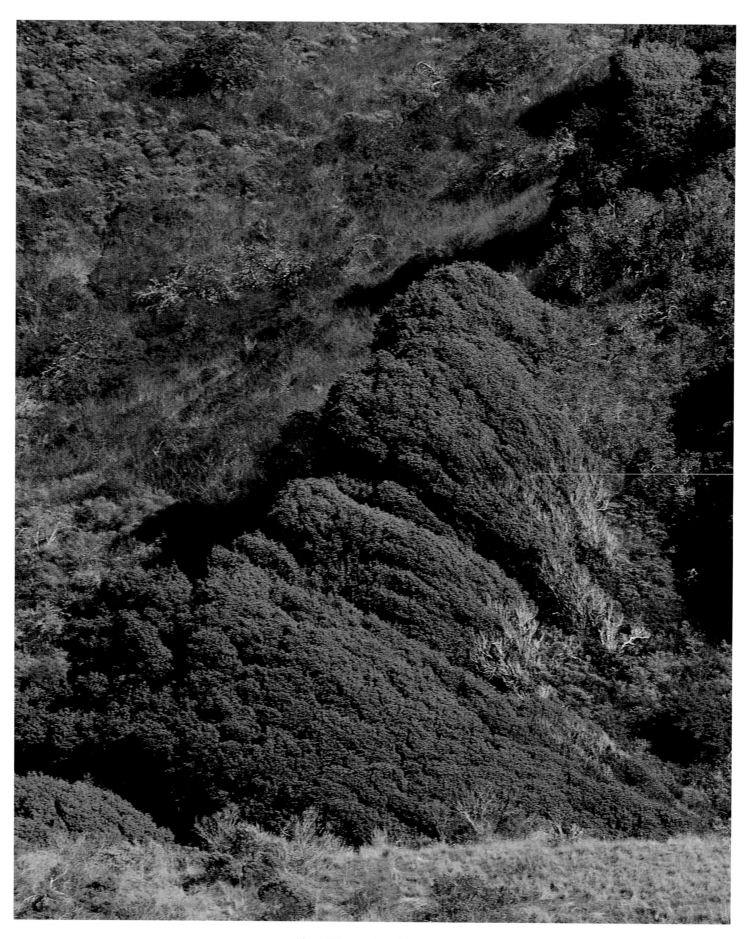

Above: Wind-sculpted trees on
property added to the Los Padres National Forest.
Right: Sunset beyond the Little Sur River and
El Sur Ranch, as seen from Highway 1.

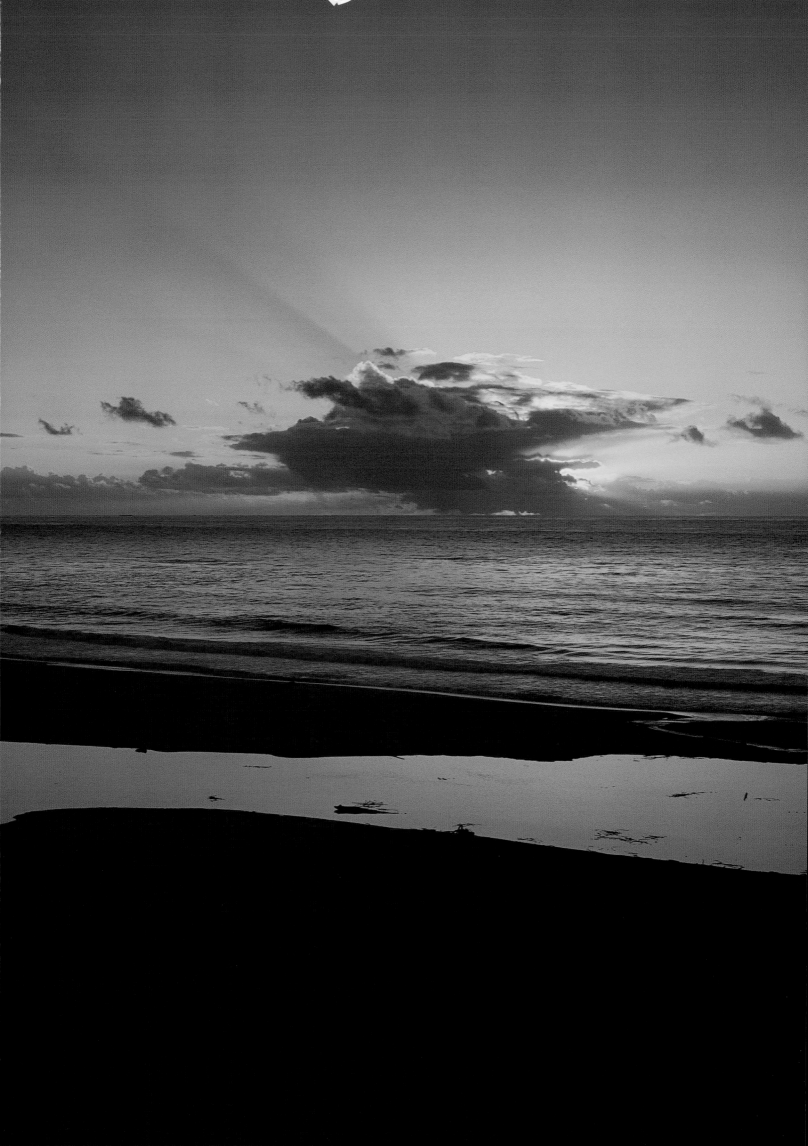

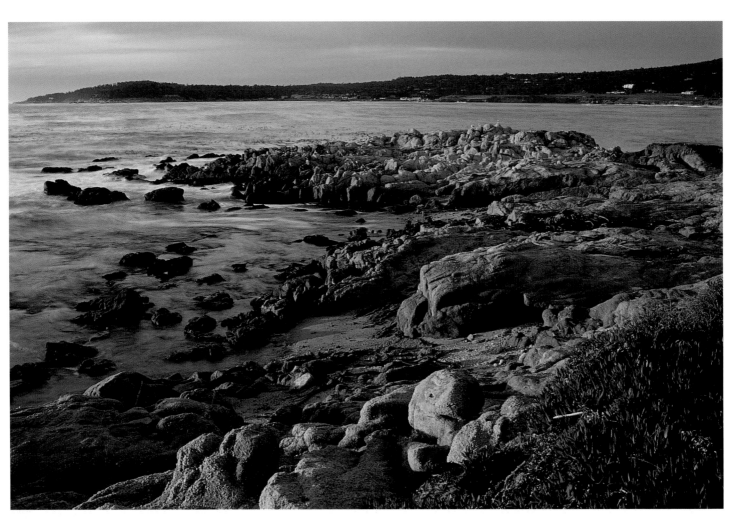

Above: Panoramic view of Pebble Beach from Carmel Point.

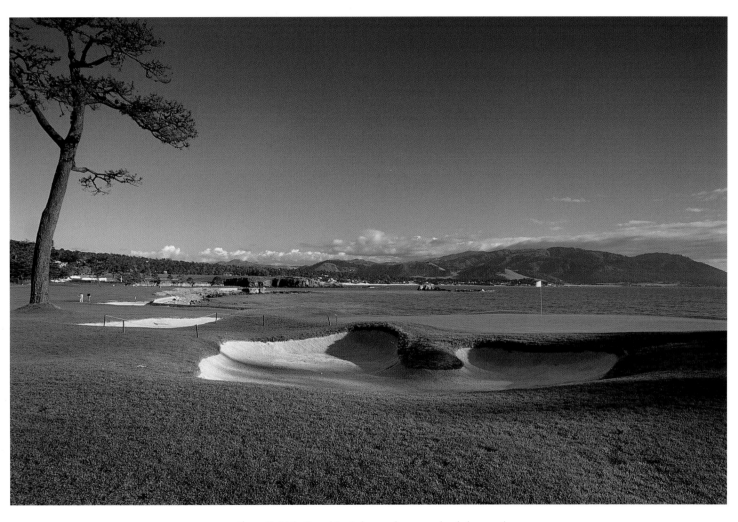

Above: Pebble Beach's eighteenth green, backdropped
by Point Lobos Ranch and Carmel Bay.

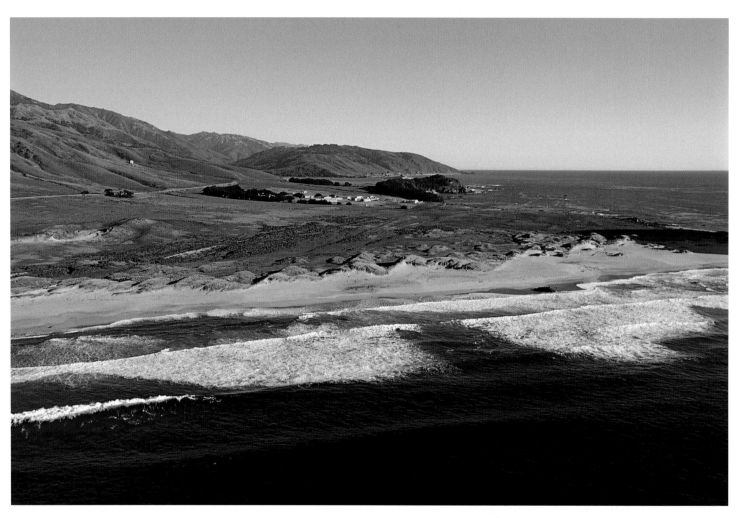

Above: El Sur Ranch from the air.

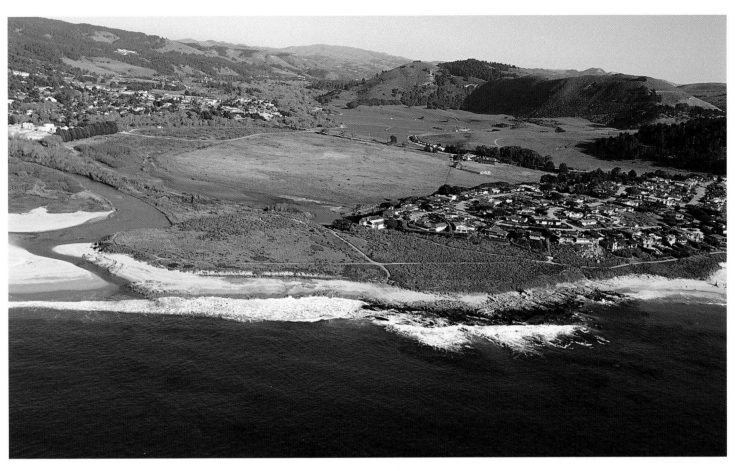

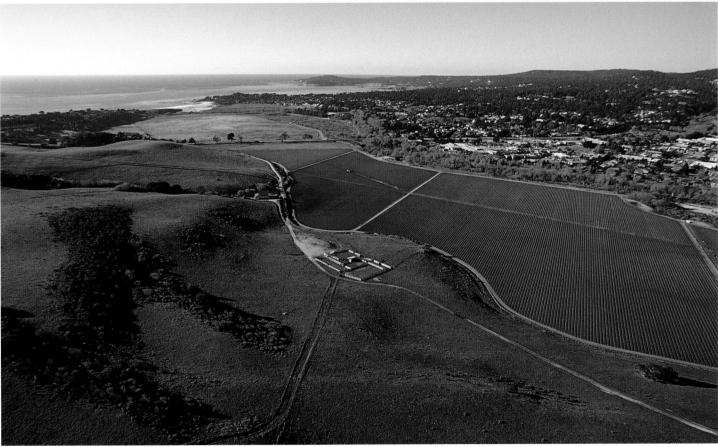

Above top: View of Carmel River State Beach and the Coast Ranch.
Above bottom: Looking west at the Coast Ranch.

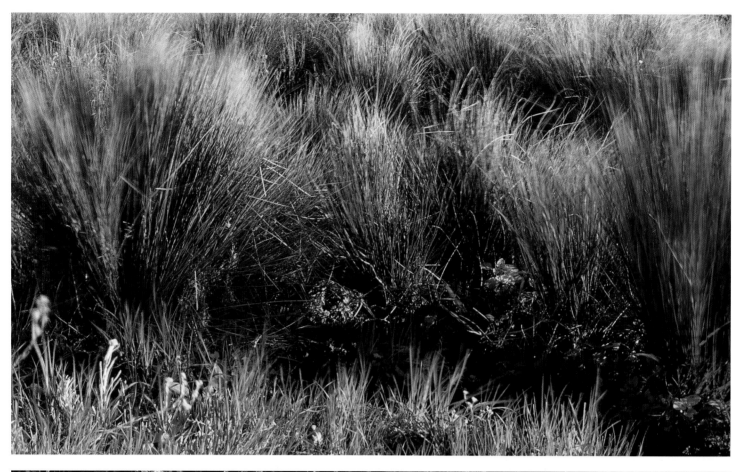

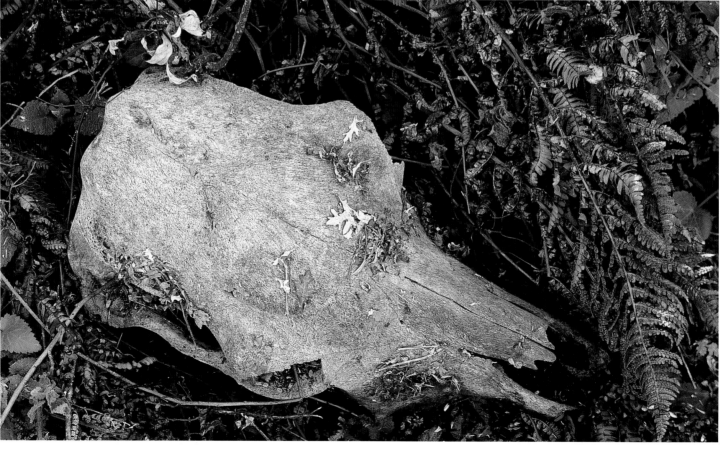

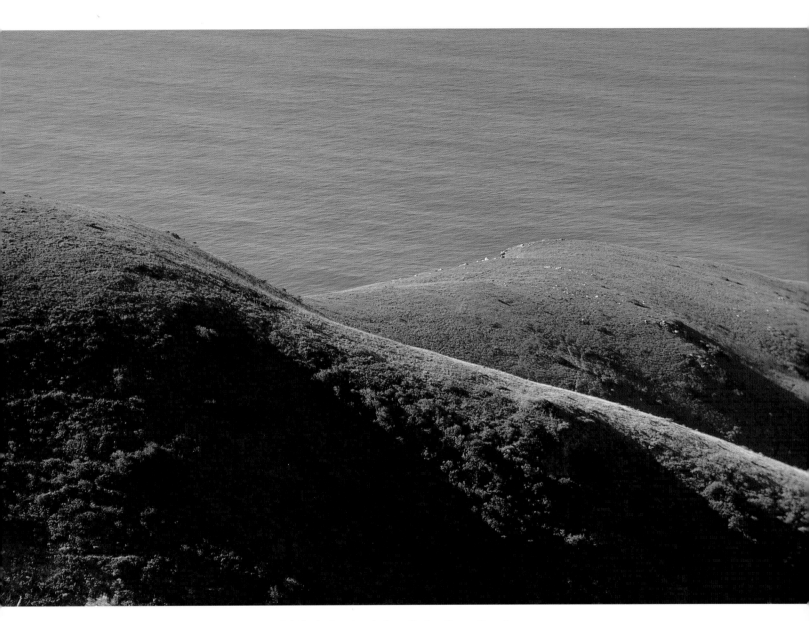

Left (both photos) and above: Bixby Ocean Ranch.

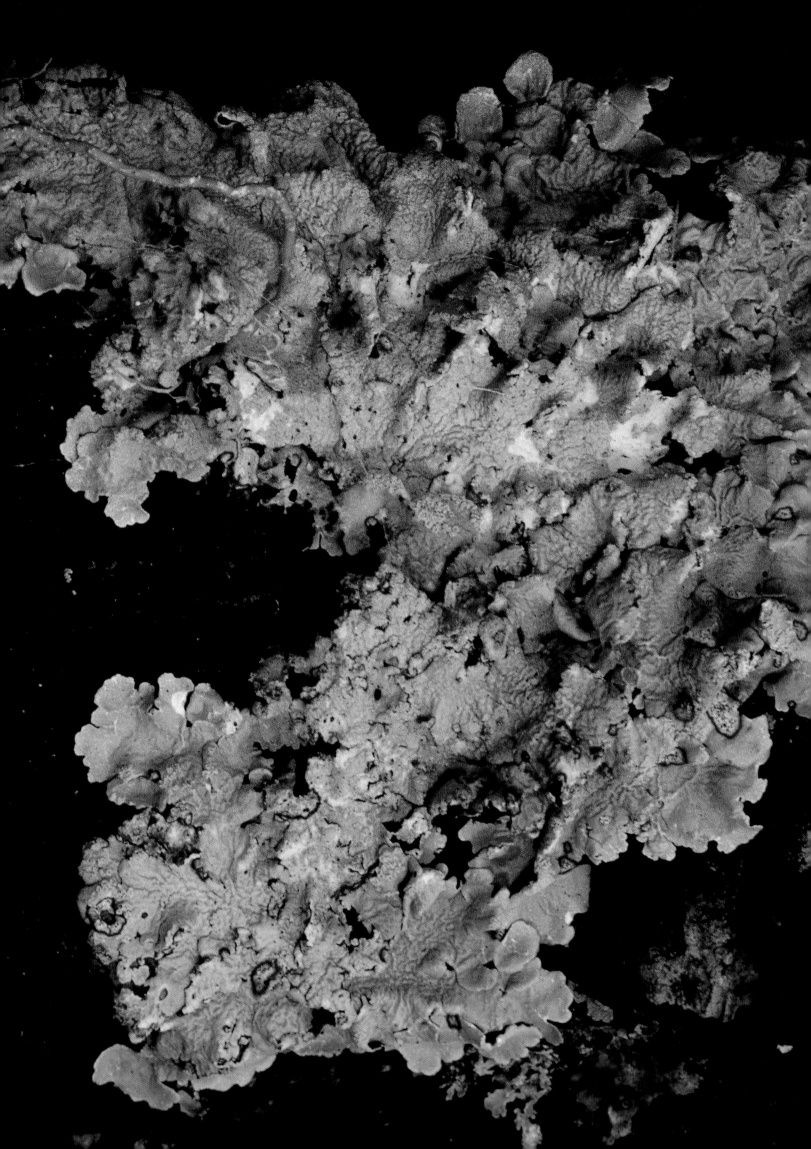

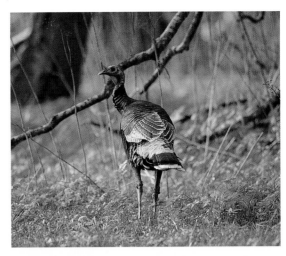

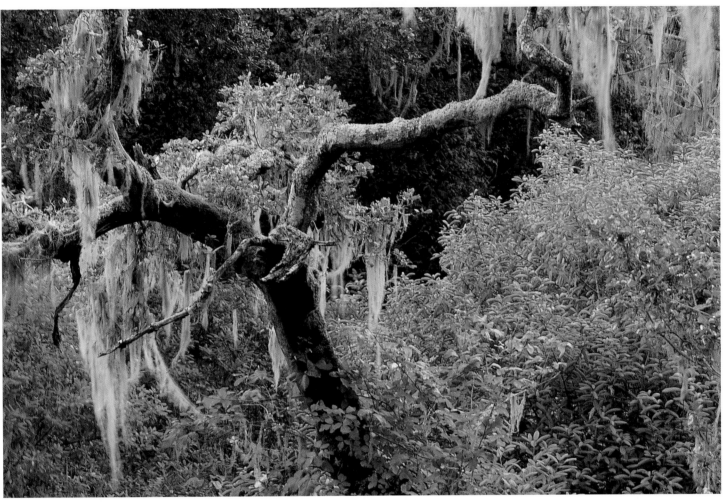

Left and above (both photos): A Monterey pine covered with fungus, a wild turkey,
and a coast live oak draped with lace lichen at the Point Lobos Ranch.
Overleaf: Intertwined madrones along Big Sur's south coast.

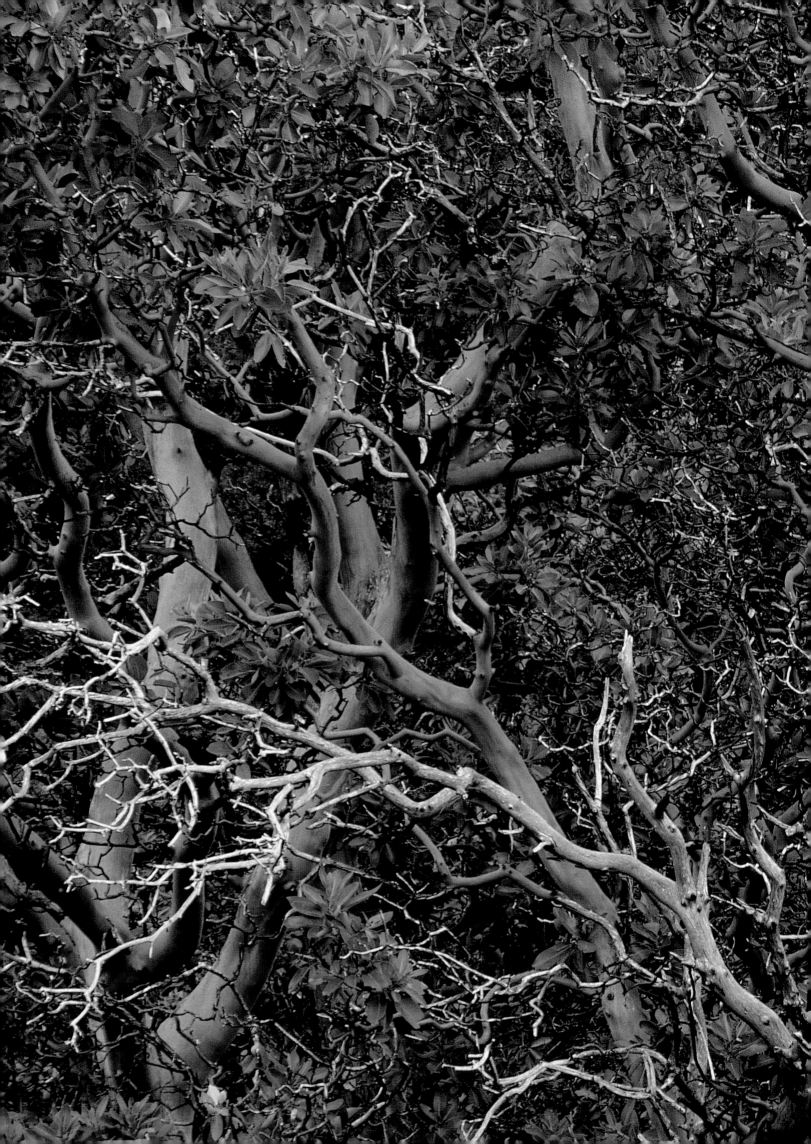

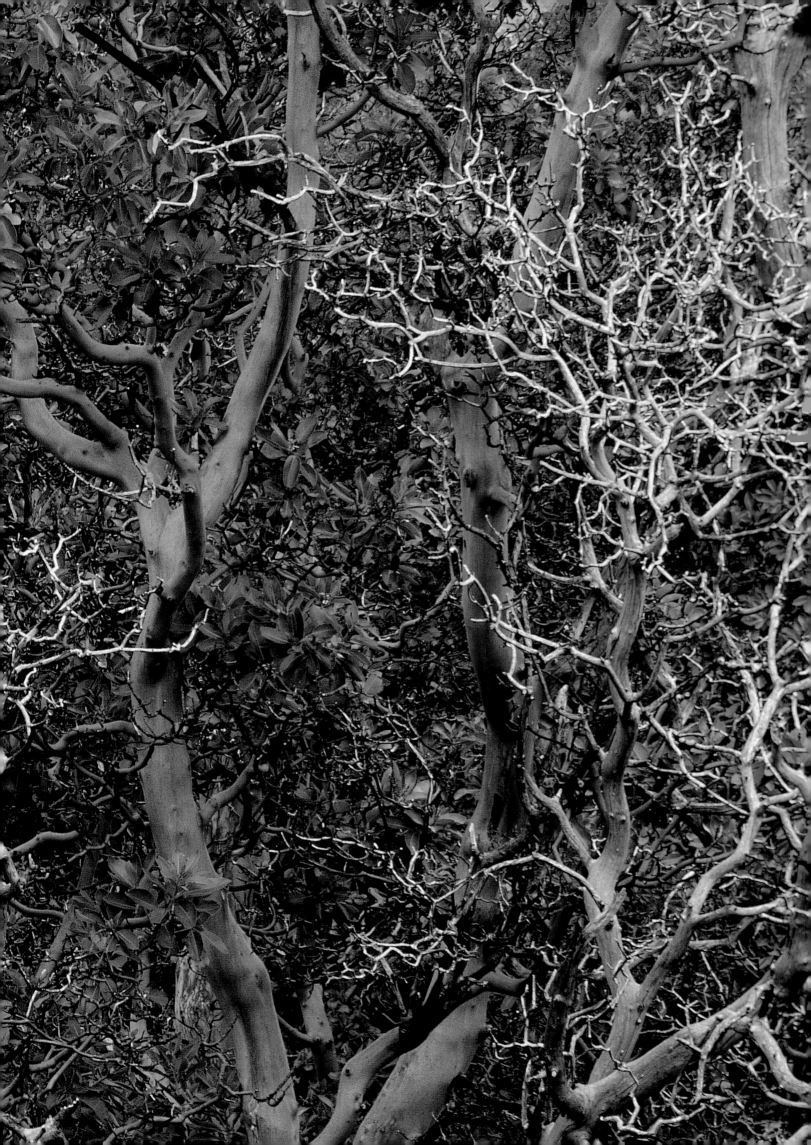

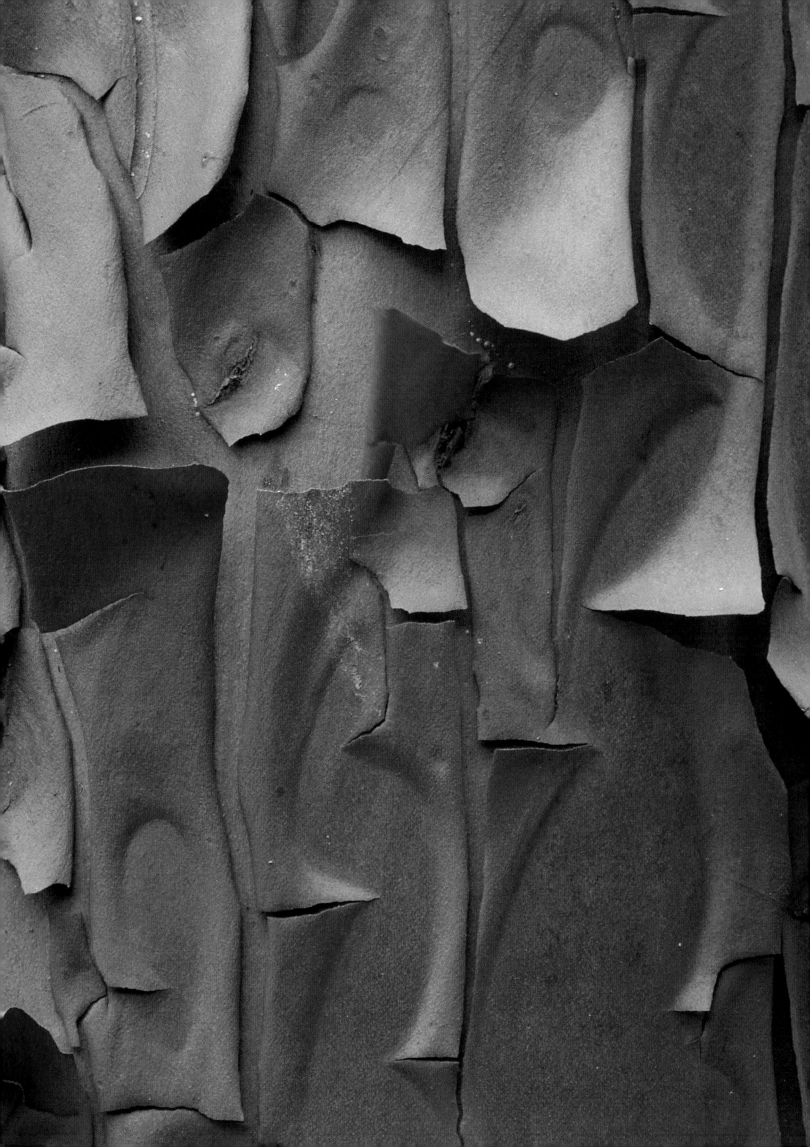

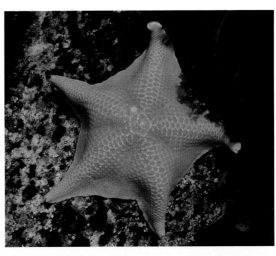

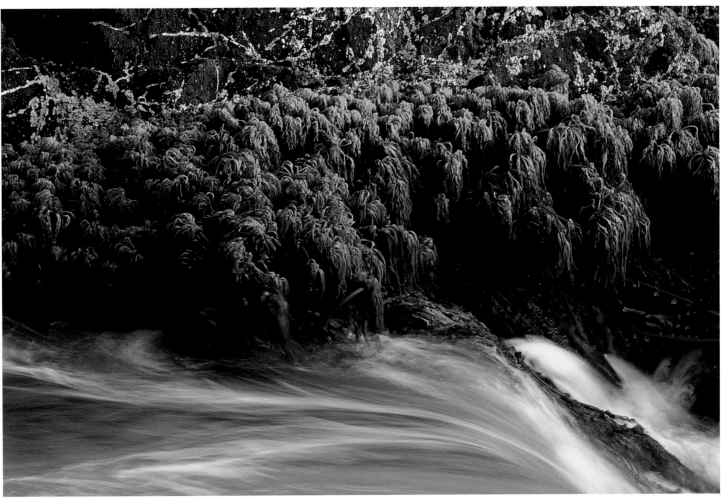

Left: Vibrant madrone bark.
Above (both photos): Sea star and sea palms at Rocky Point at low tide.
Overleaf: Stunning view of the El Sur Ranch from the Old Coast Road.

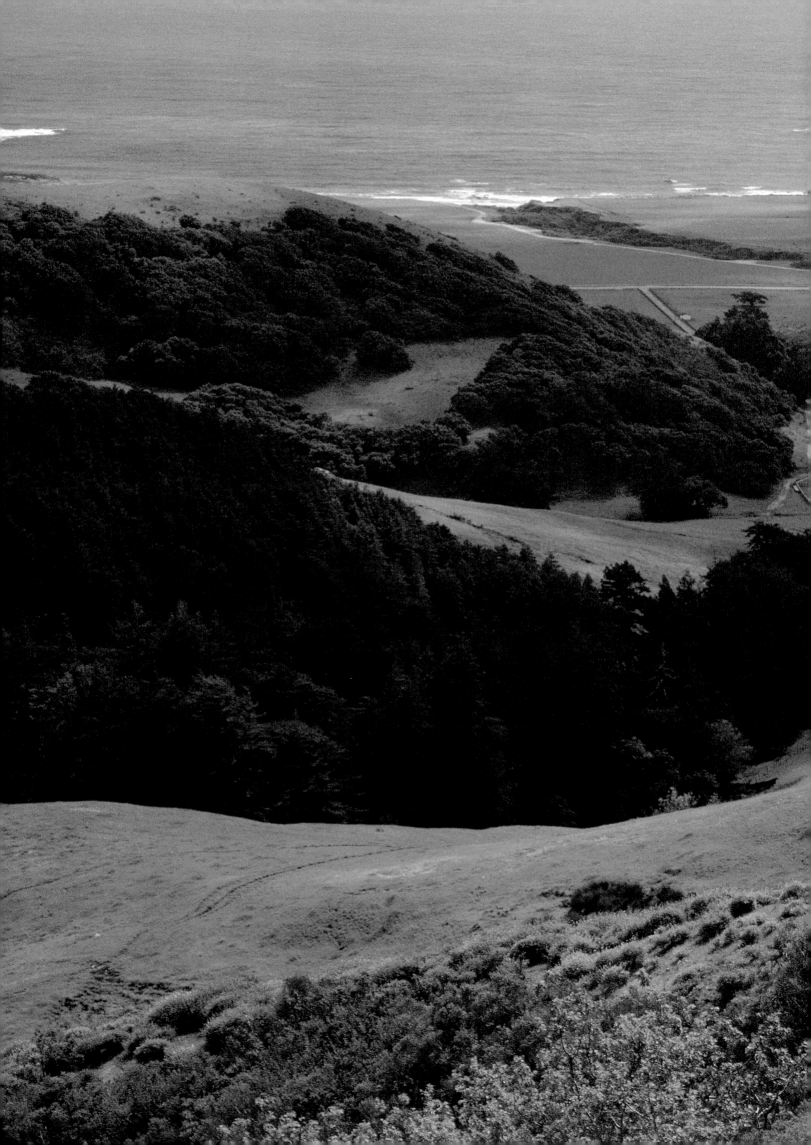

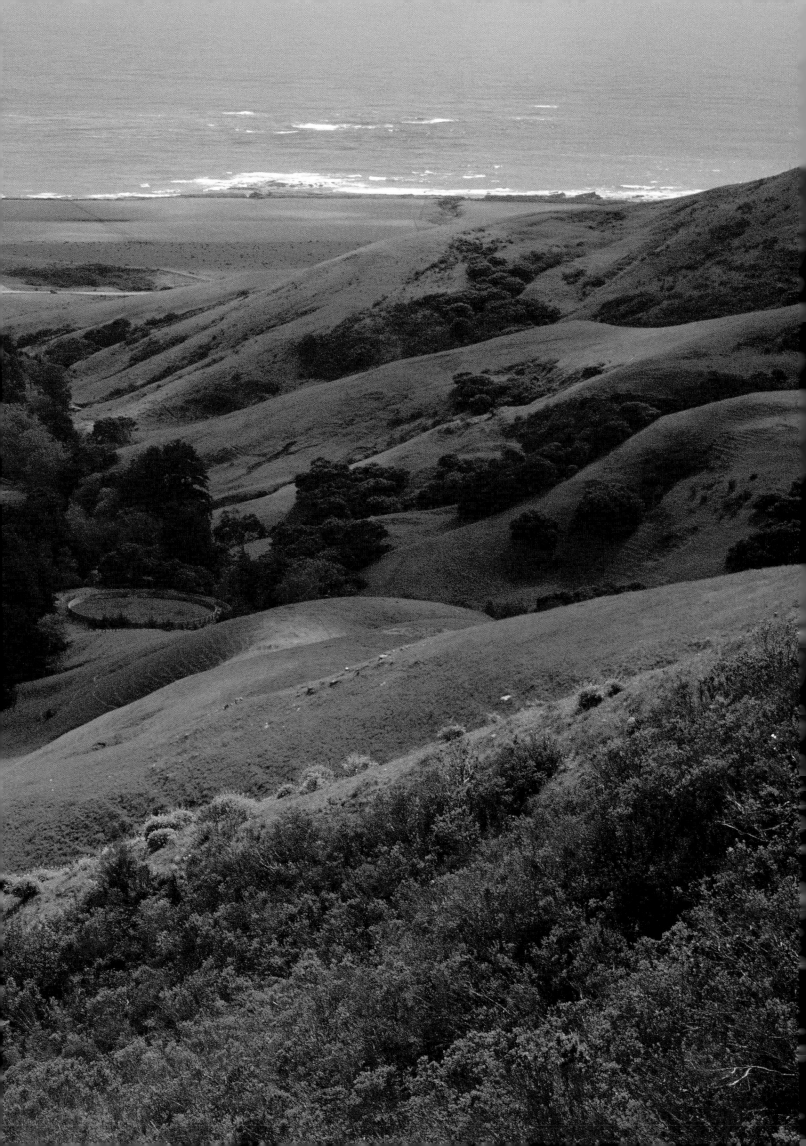

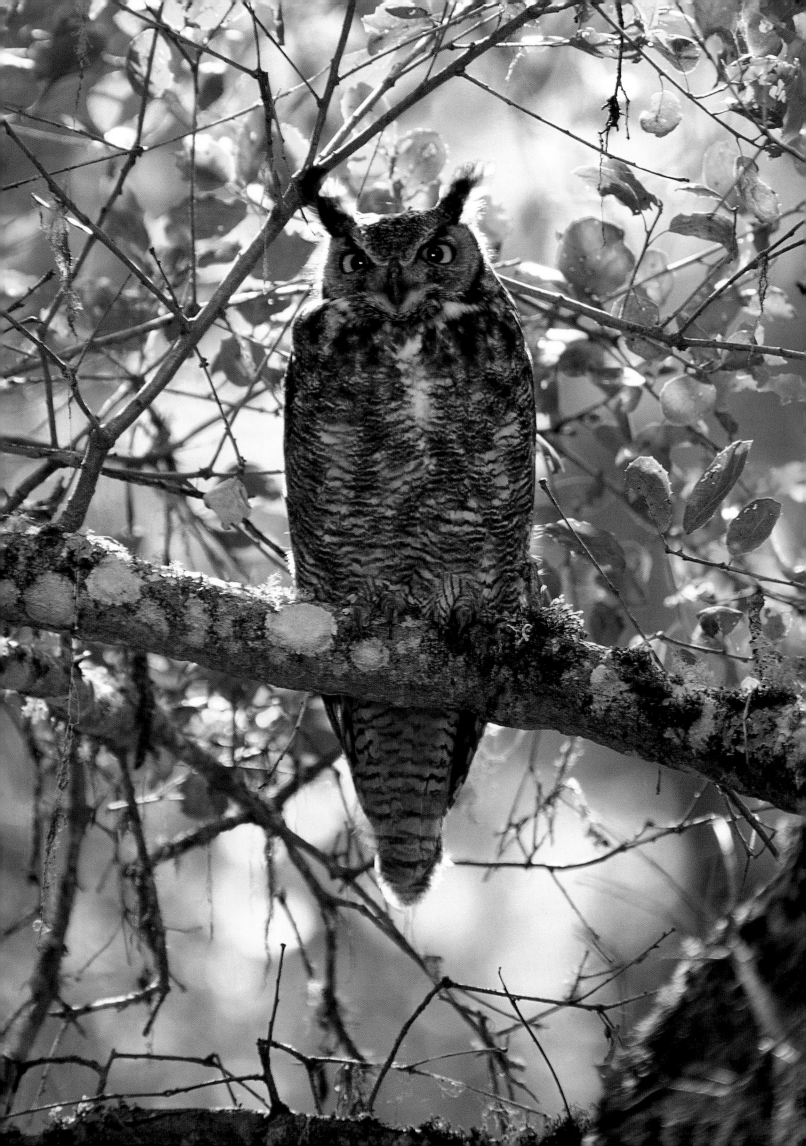

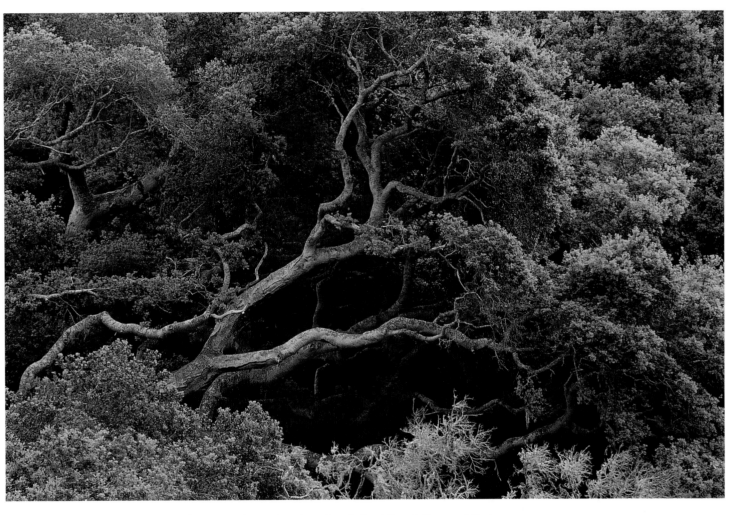

Left: A great horned owl on the Garland Ranch Regional Park expansion.
Above: Windblown coast live oaks at Point Lobos Ranch.

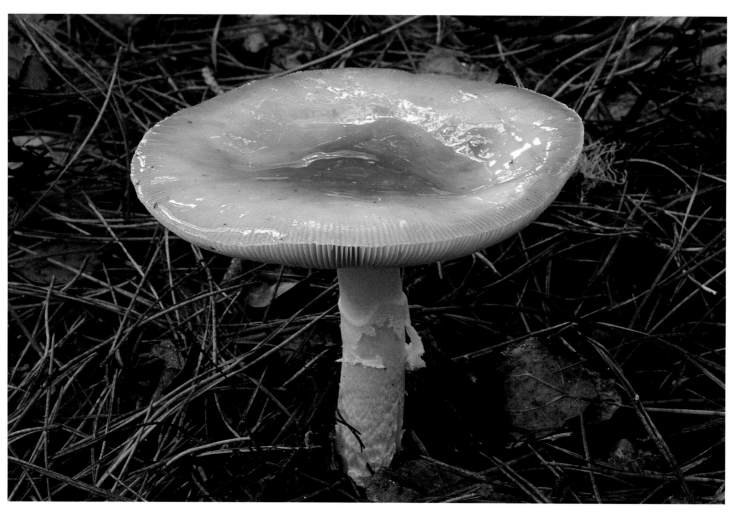

Above: Vivid mushroom at Point Lobos Ranch.
Right: Fungus on decomposing redwood at the Mill Creek Preserve.

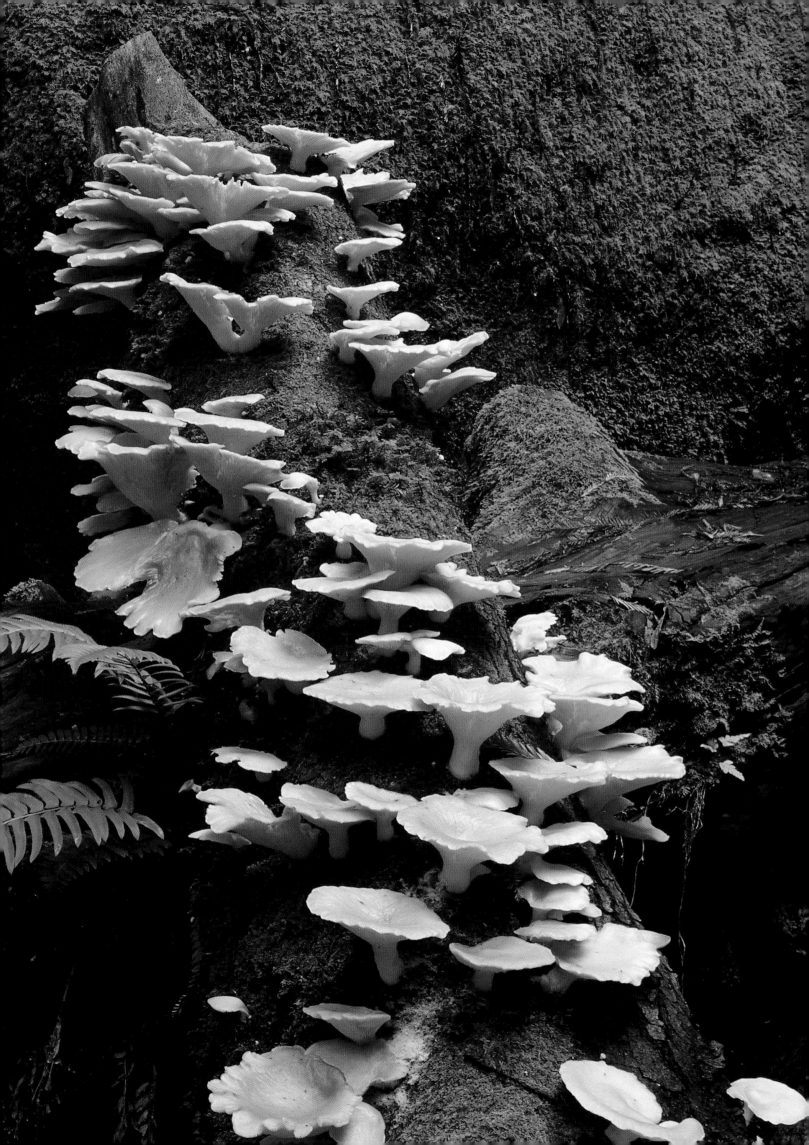

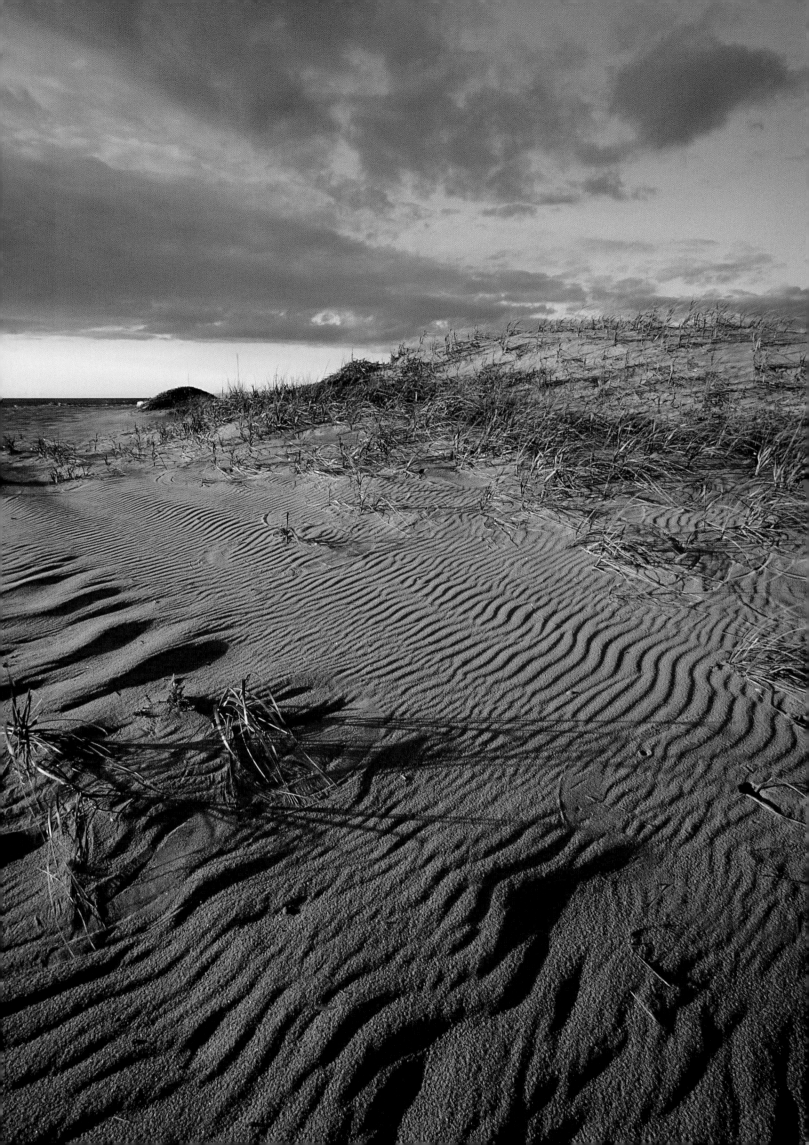

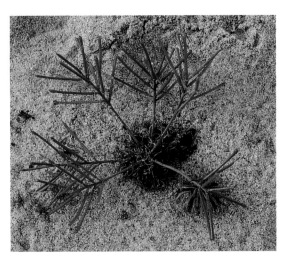

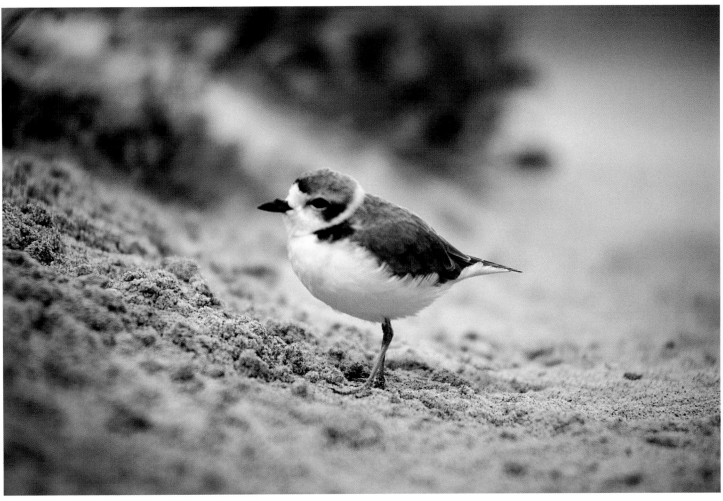

Left: Evening shadows at the Martin Dunes.
Above top: Dry seed pods of coast wallflower at Granite Rock Dunes.
Above bottom: The snowy plover, listed as threatened by the federal government,
often found in habitat preserved along the Monterey Bay State Seashore.
Overleaf: A dry yucca plant at Mill Creek Preserve.

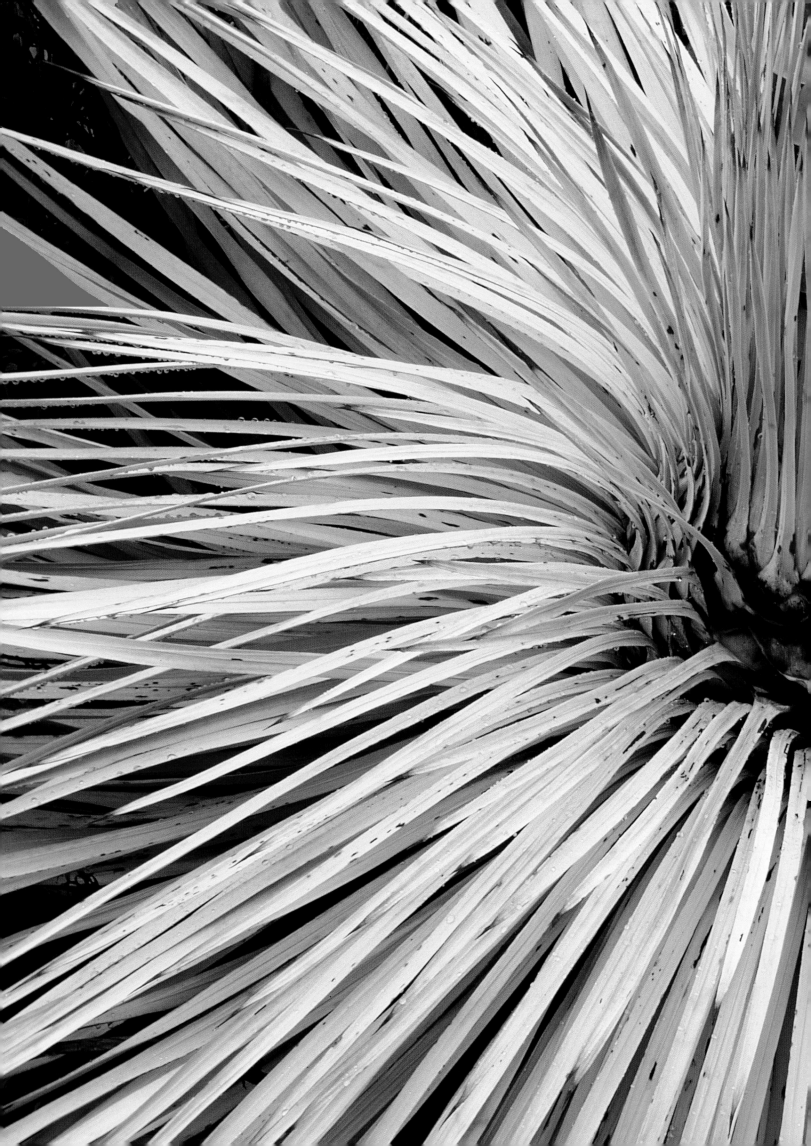

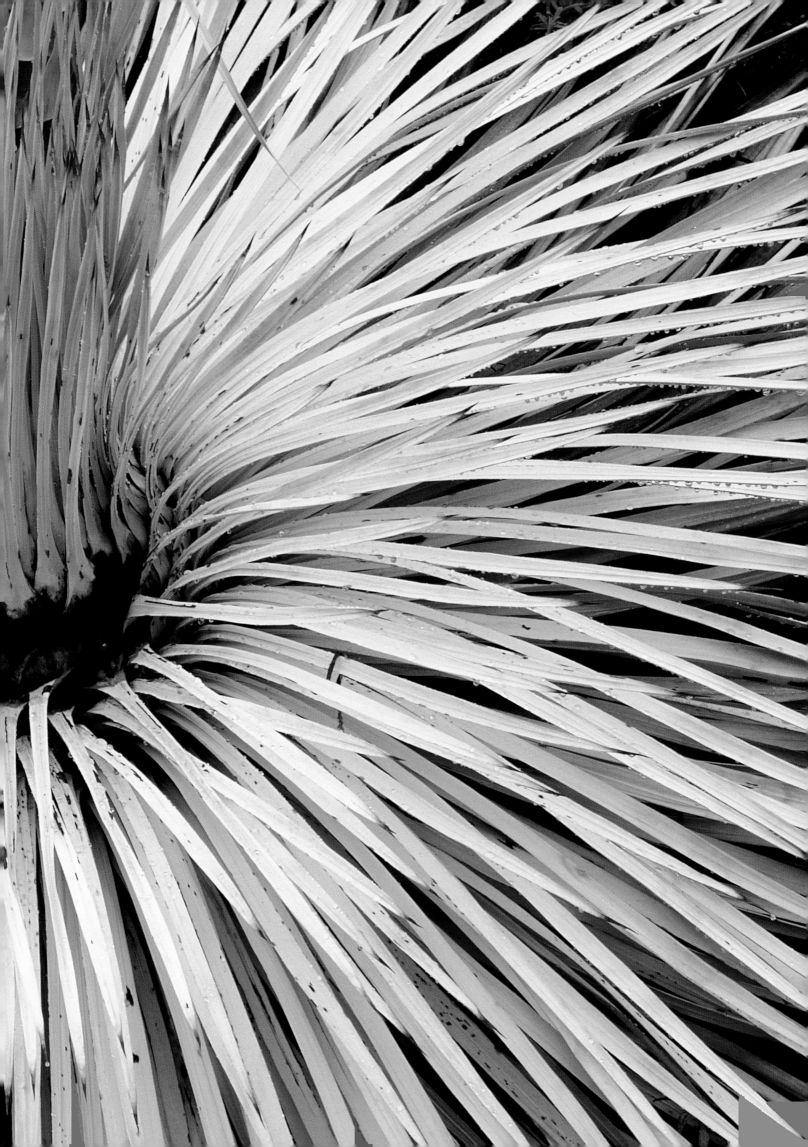

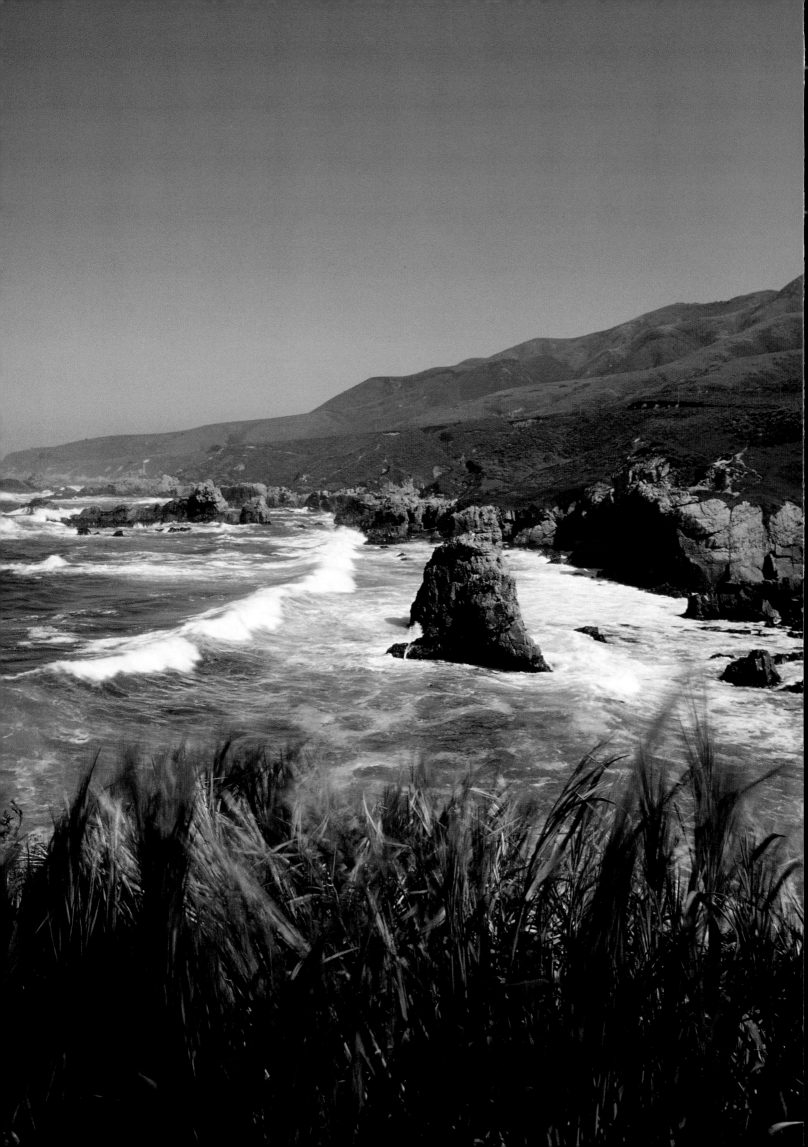

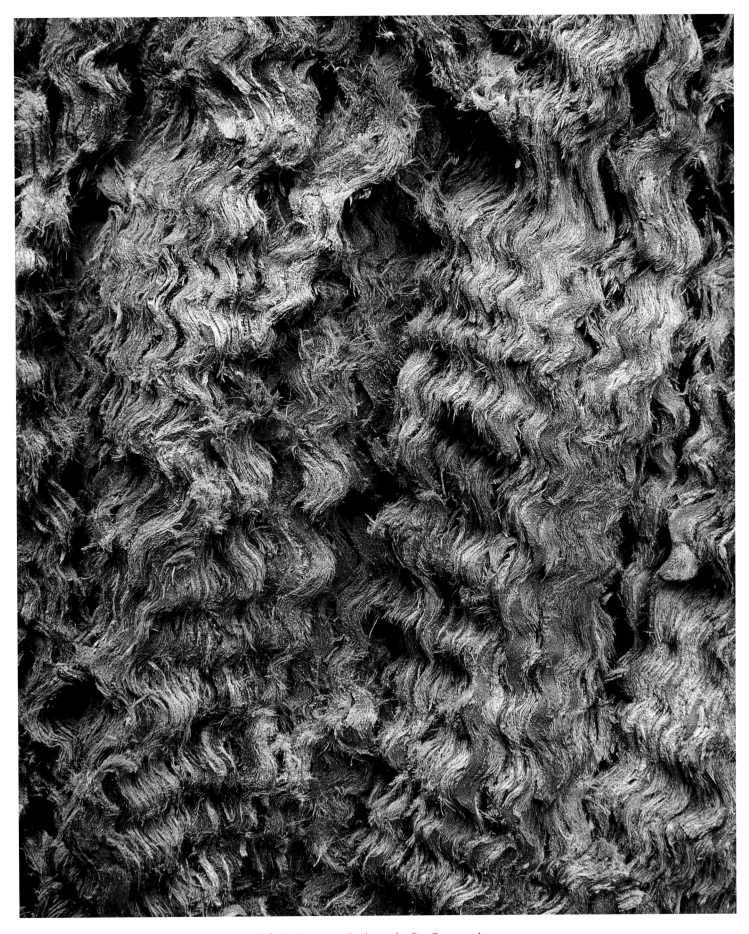

Left: Looking north along the Big Sur coastline.
Above: Wavy redwood bark in Los Padres National Forest addition.

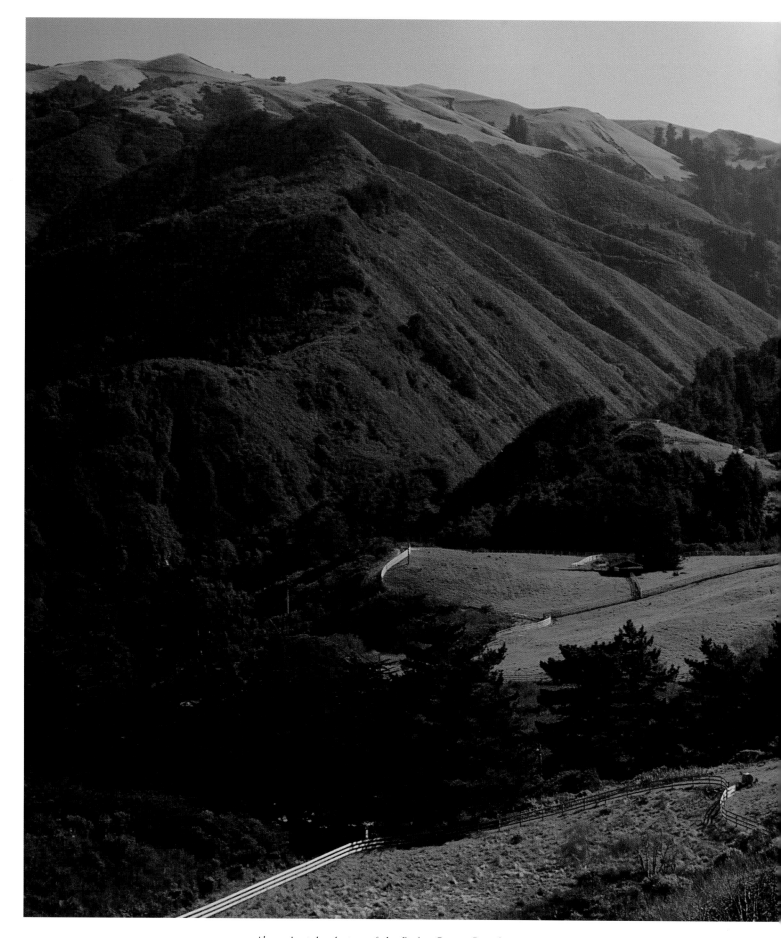

Above: An inland view of the Bixby Ocean Ranch.

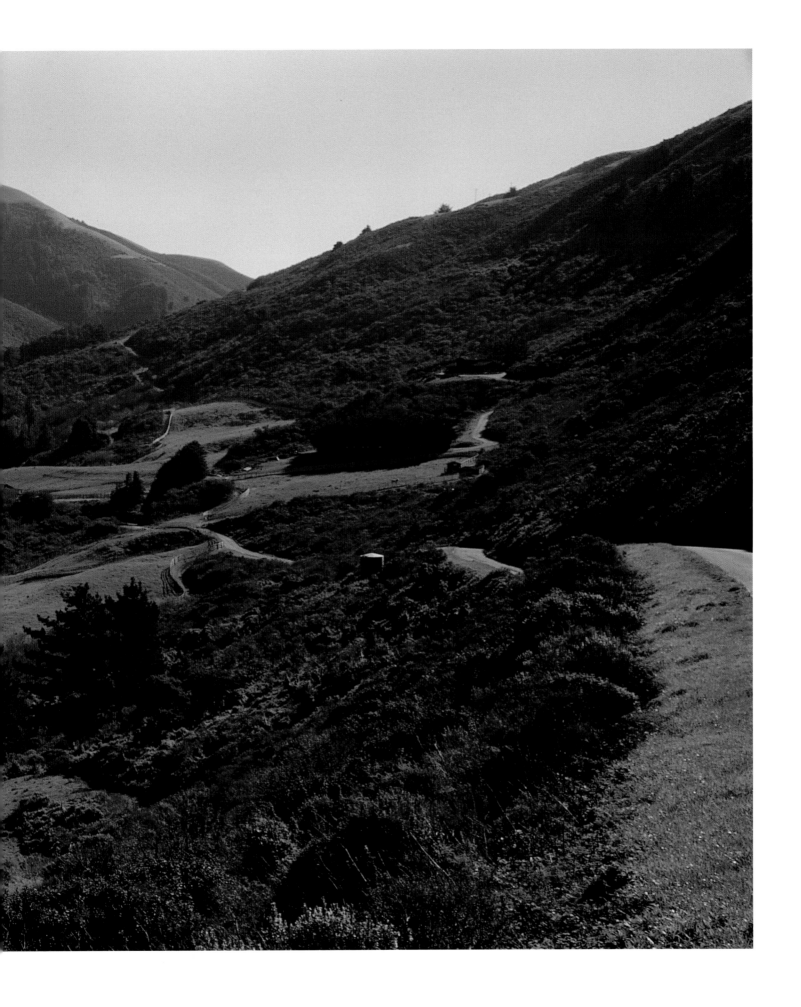

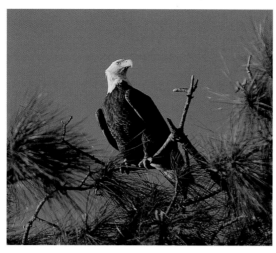

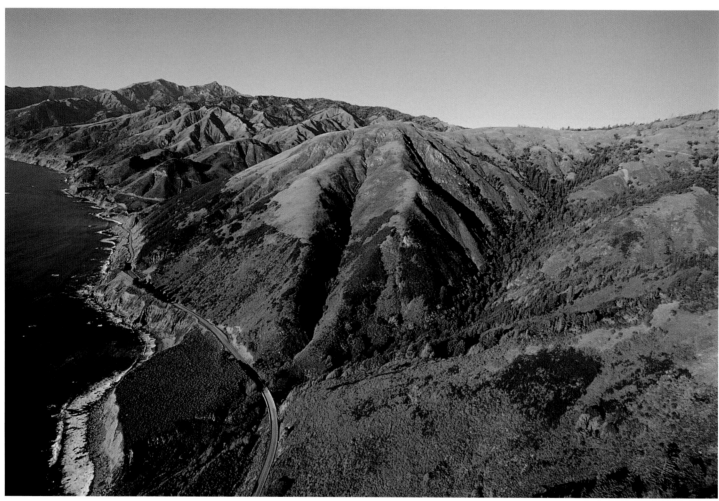

Above (both photos): Bald eagle, once extinct in the area, now successfully reintroduced to the Big Sur coastal region.
Right: The beach below Bixby Ocean Ranch.

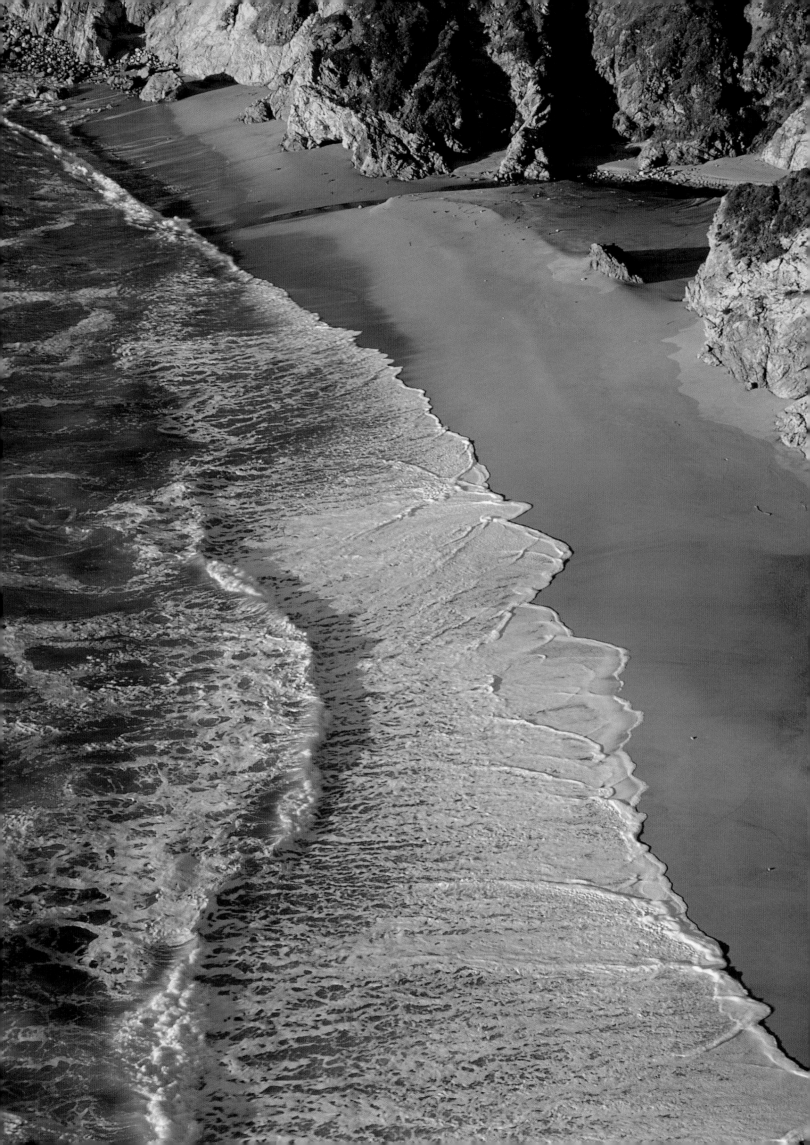

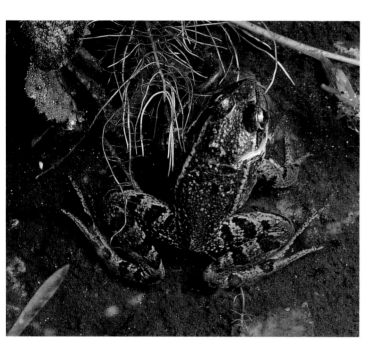

Above: A California red-legged frog, on the
federal government's list of threatened and
endangered species, protected along the
San Jose Creek on the Point Lobos Ranch.
Right: Williams Creek and old-growth
redwood forest on the Mitteldorf Preserve.

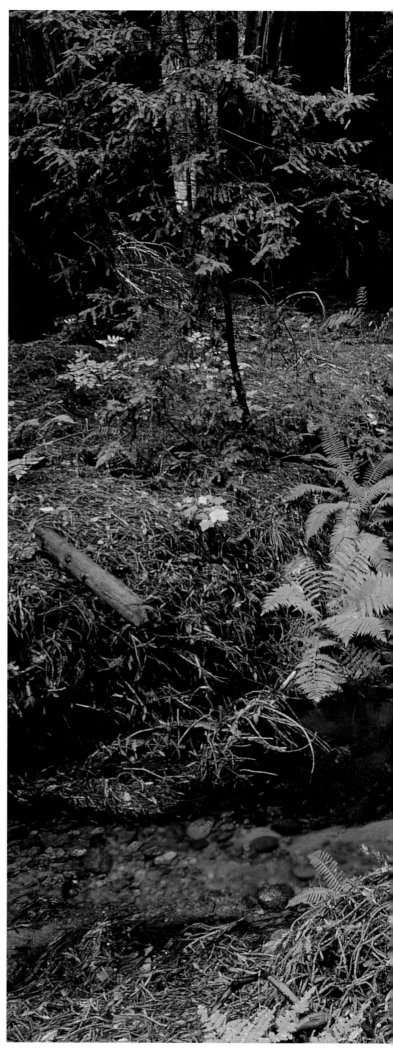

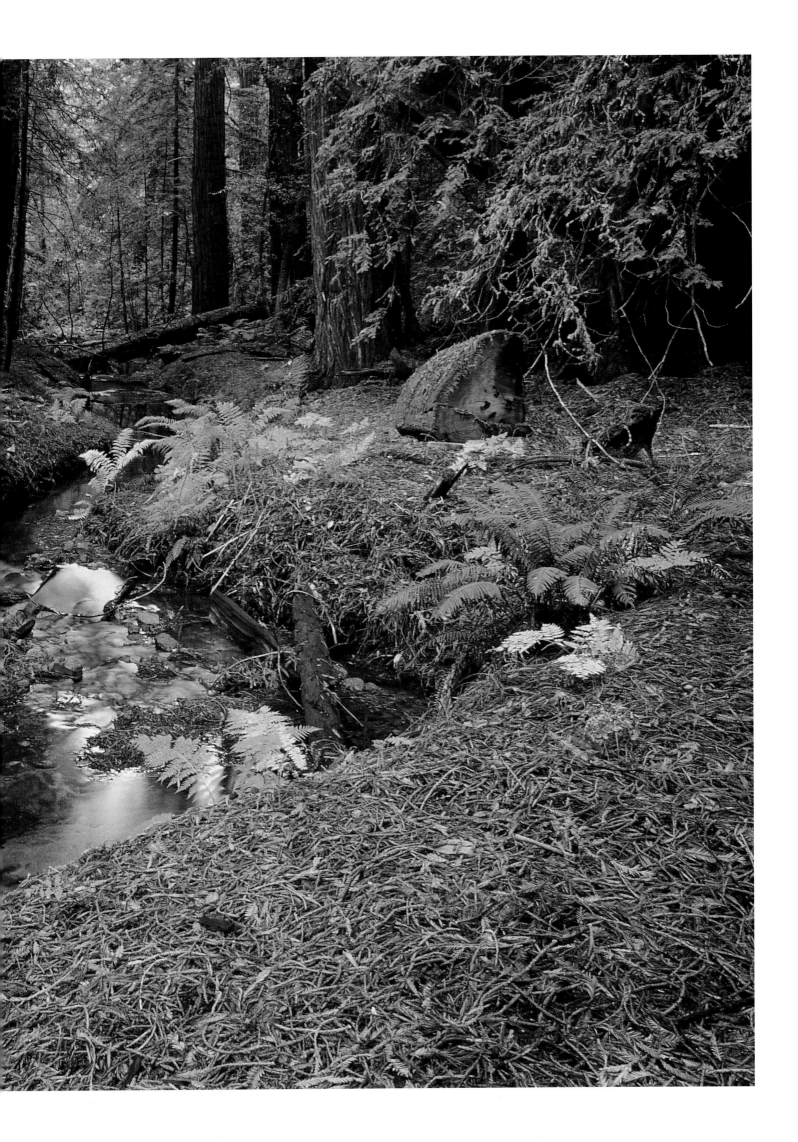

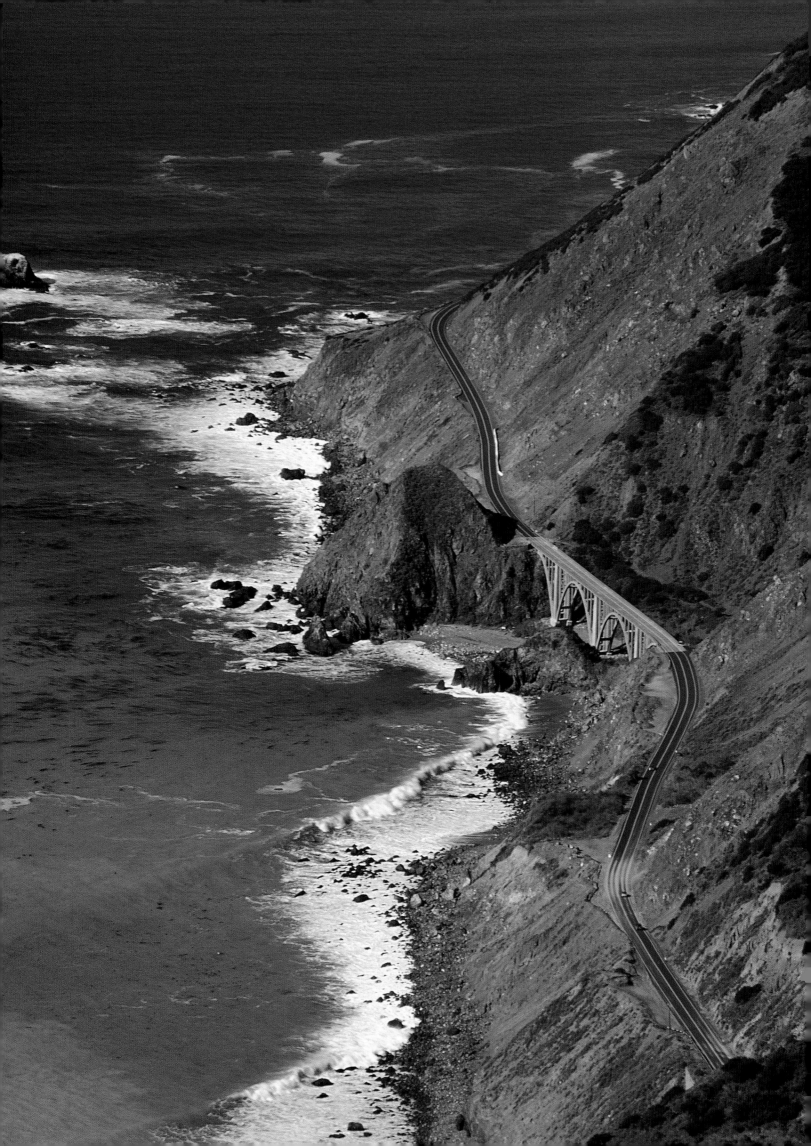

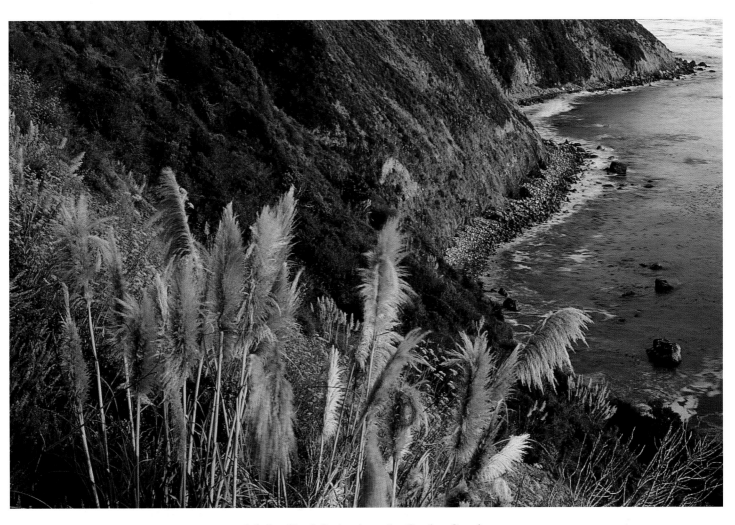

Left: Big Creek Bridge from the Gamboa Ranch.
Above: Pampas grass, a nonnative invader
of large areas along the Big Sur Coast.

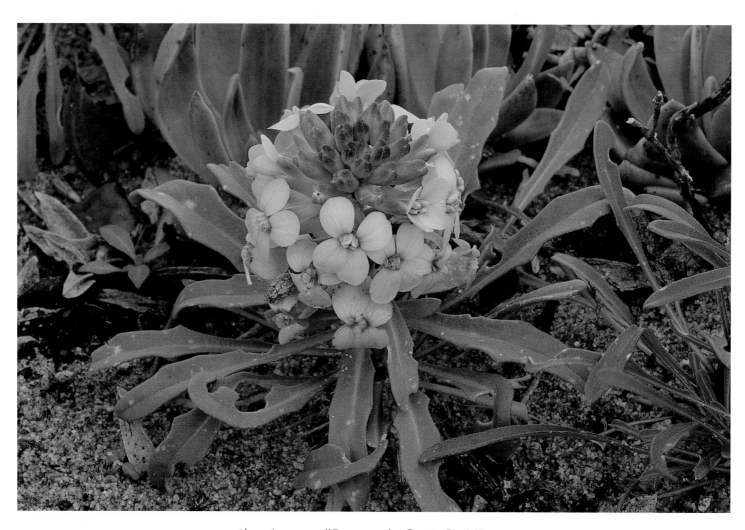

Above: A coast wallflower on the Granite Rock Dunes.

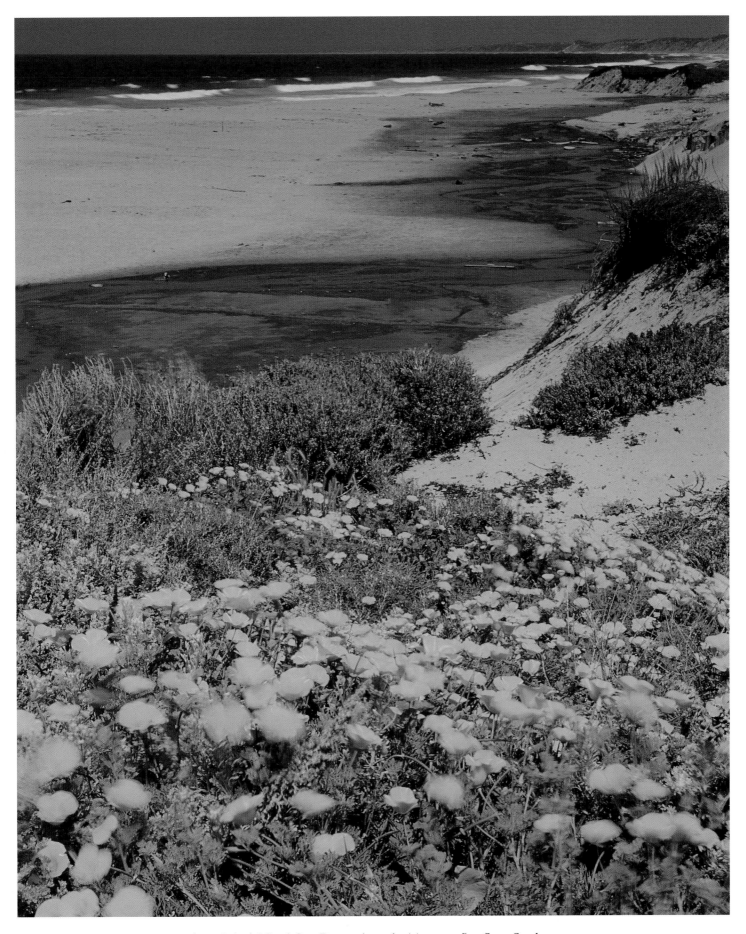

Above: Colorful Sand City Dunes along the Monterey Bay State Seashore.

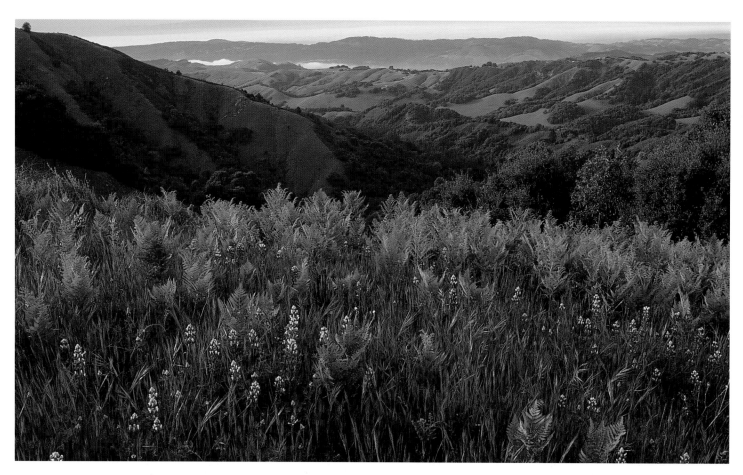

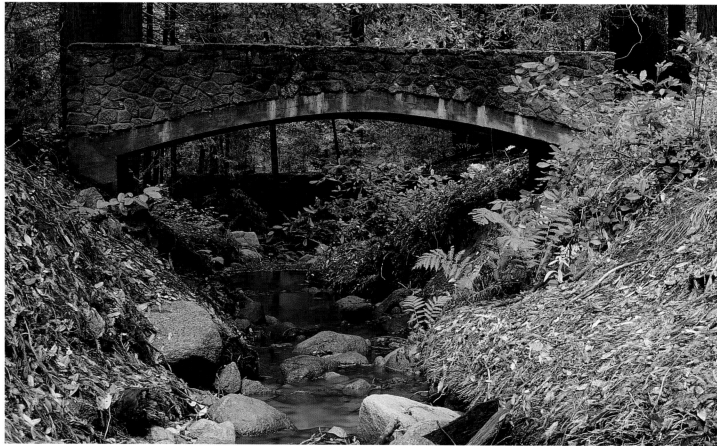

Above (both photos) and right: Views of the Mitteldorf Preserve.
Overleaf: Landels–Hill Big Creek Reserve as seen from Gamboa Point.

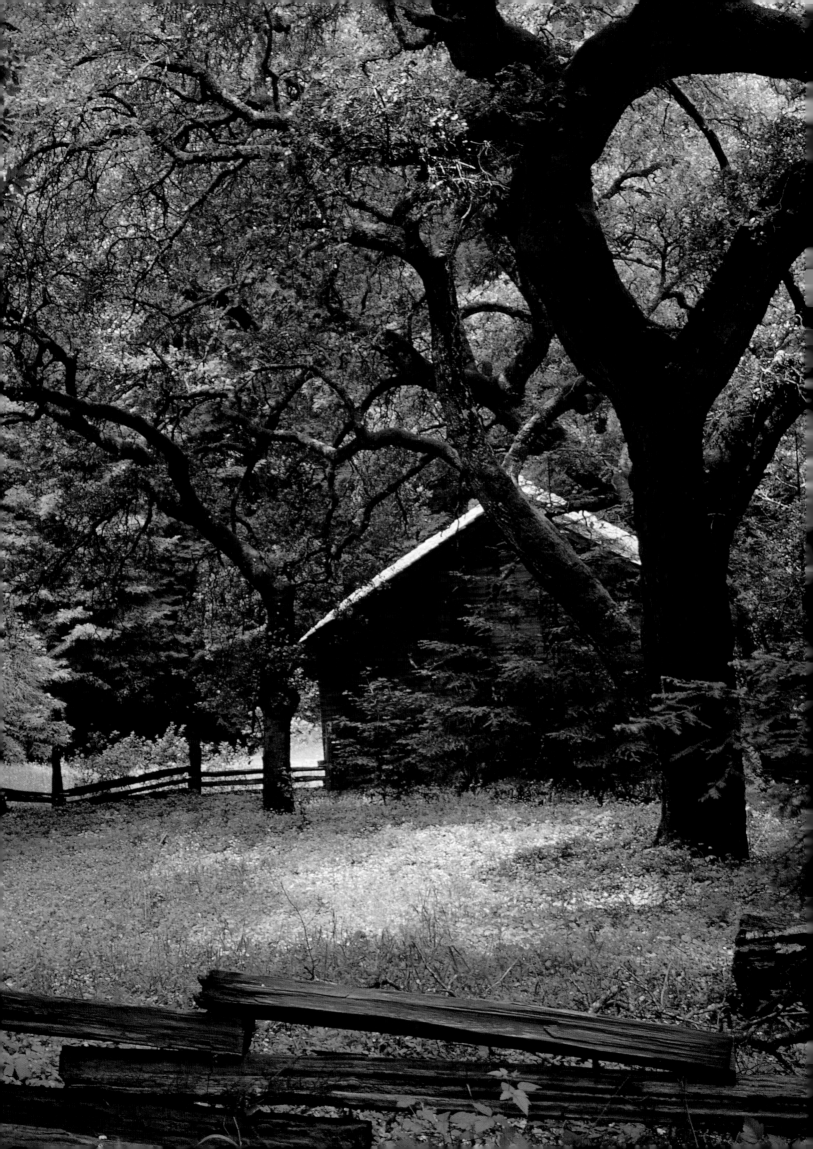

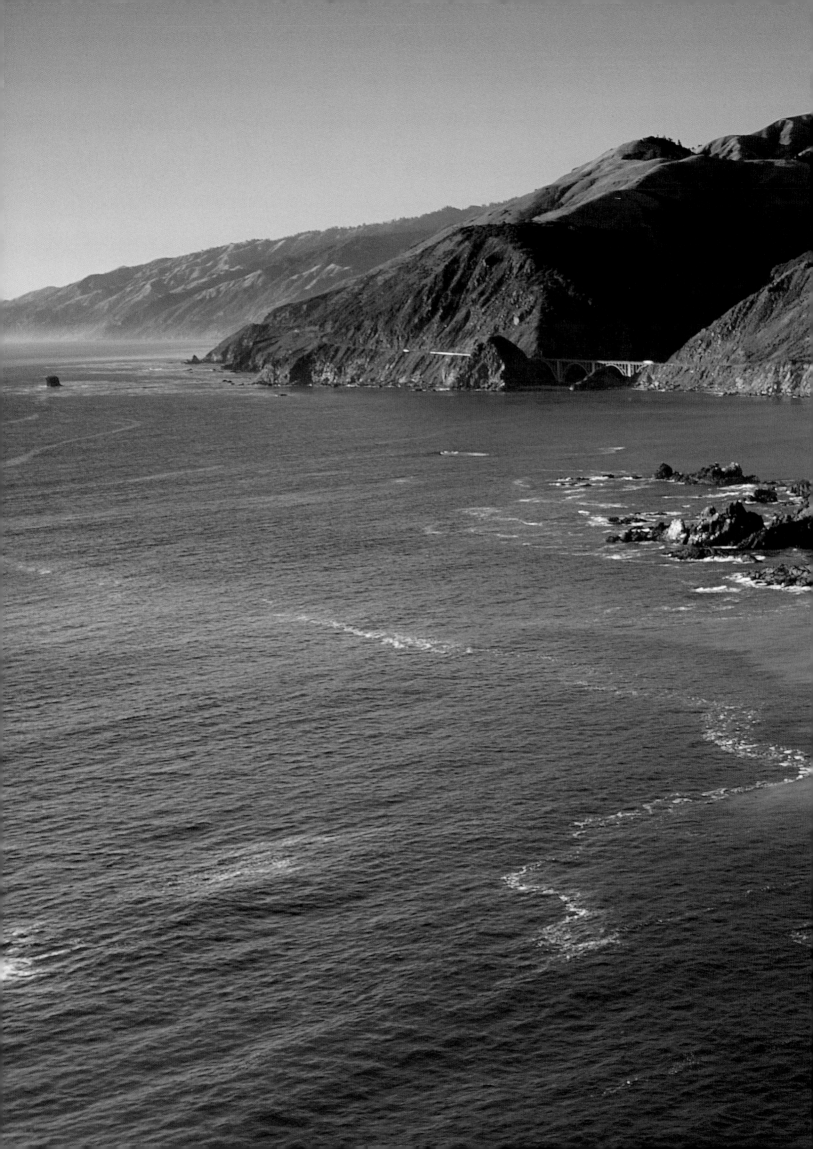

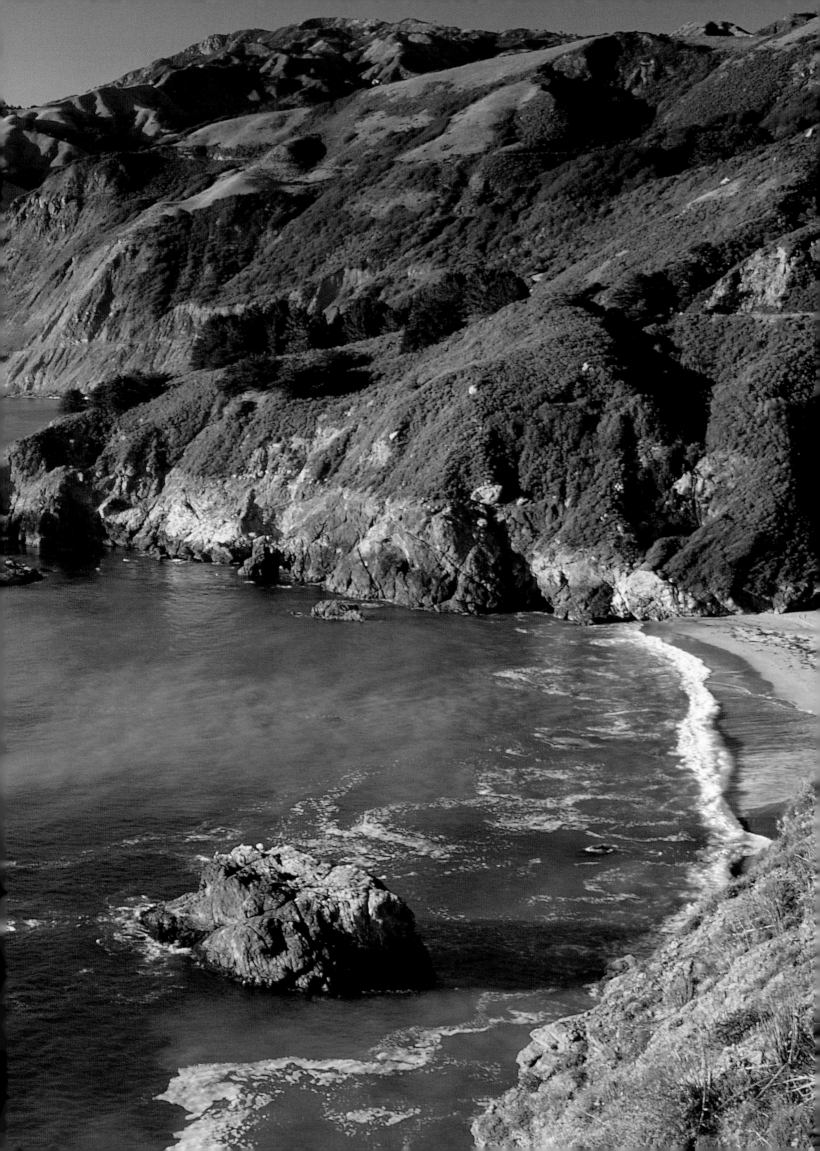

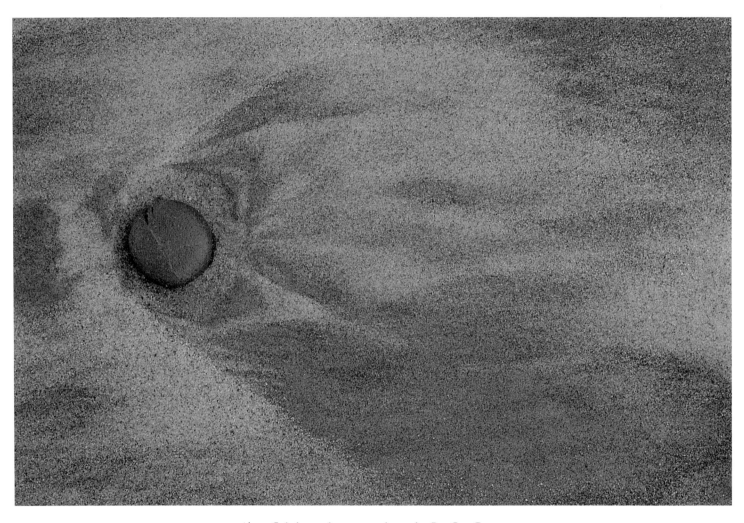

Above: Subtle sand patterns along the Big Sur Coast.
Right: Poison oak in autumn at Garland Ranch Regional Park expansion.
Overleaf: Celebrated Point Lobos State Reserve and the Point Lobos Ranch.

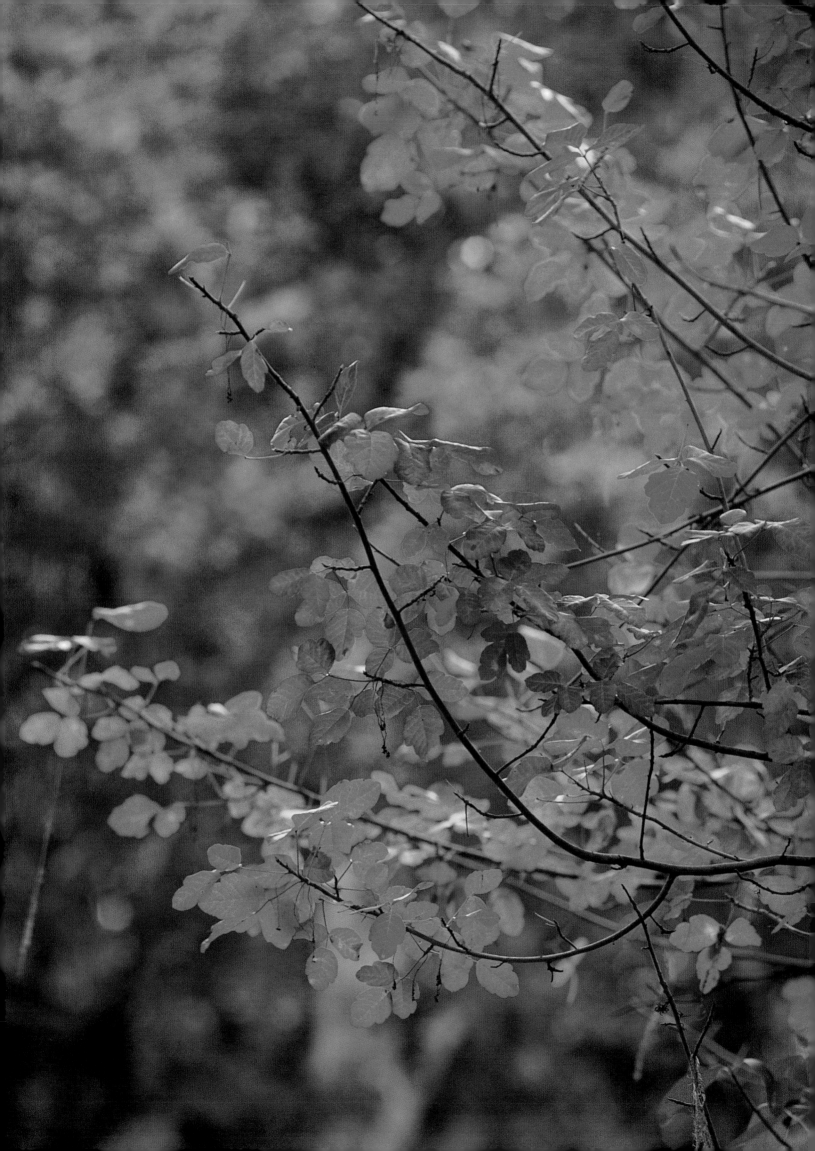

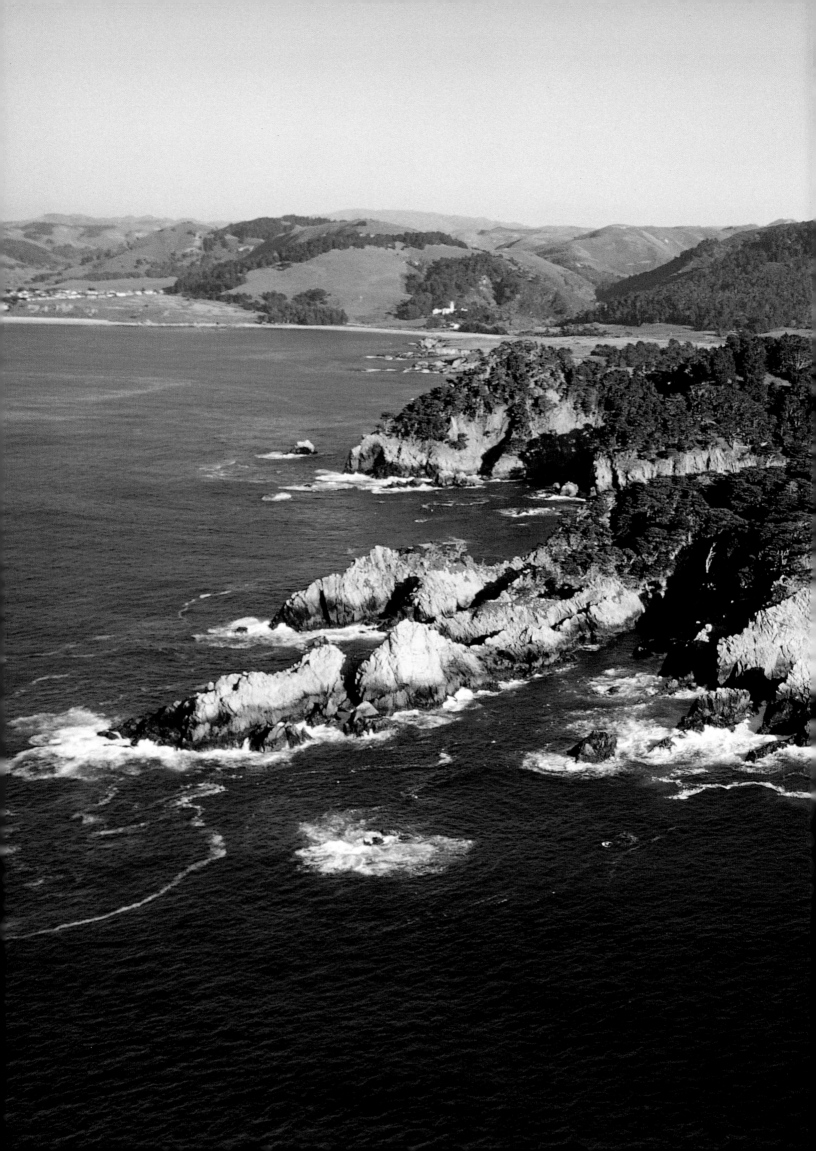

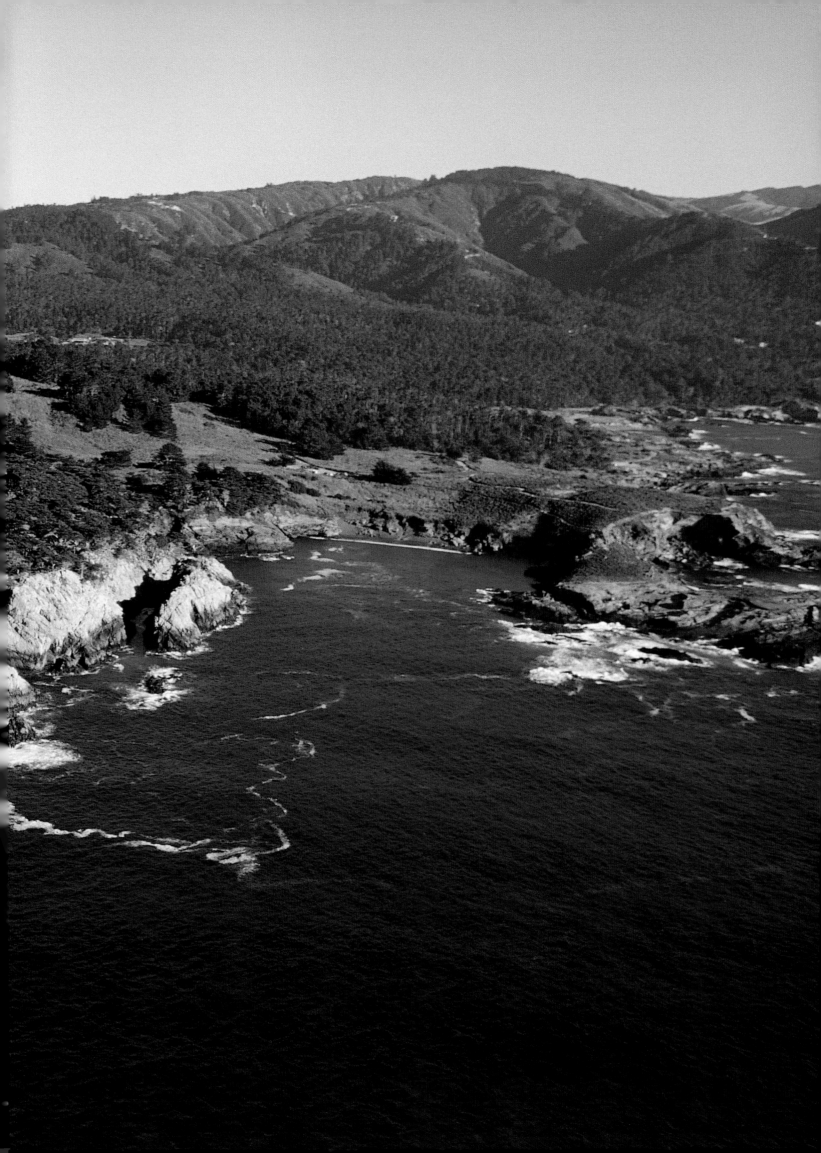

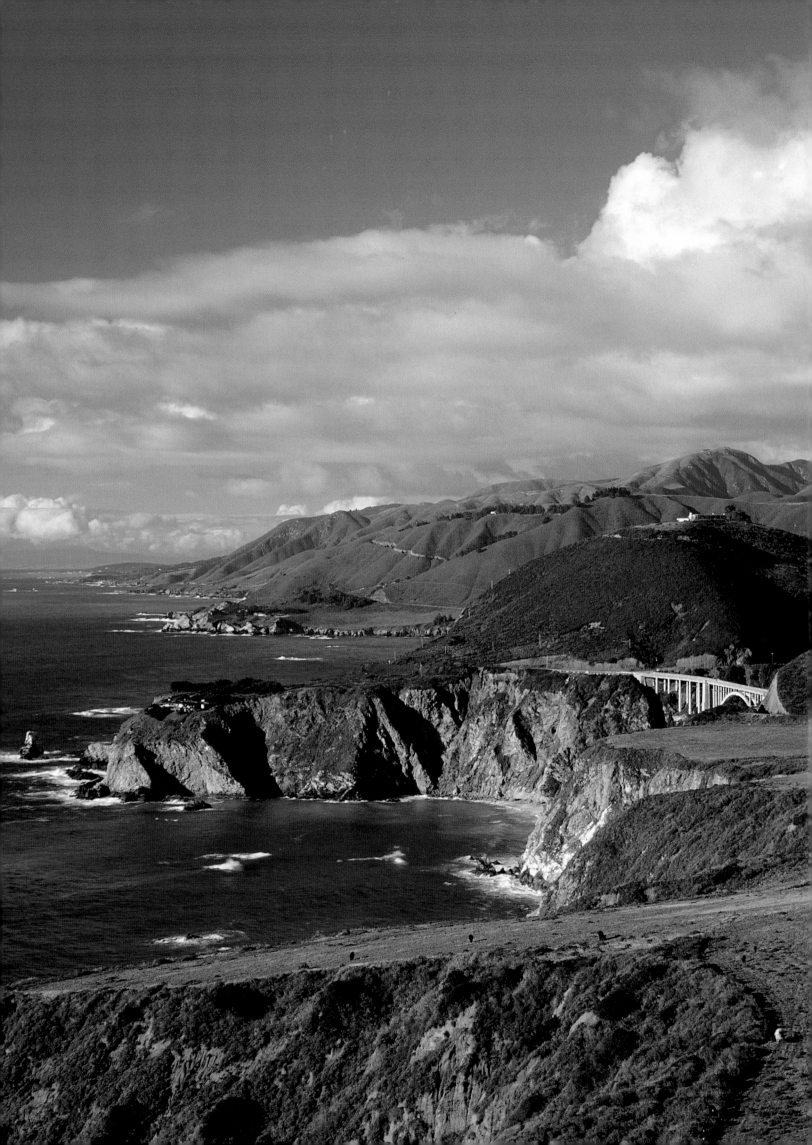

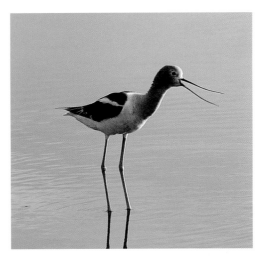

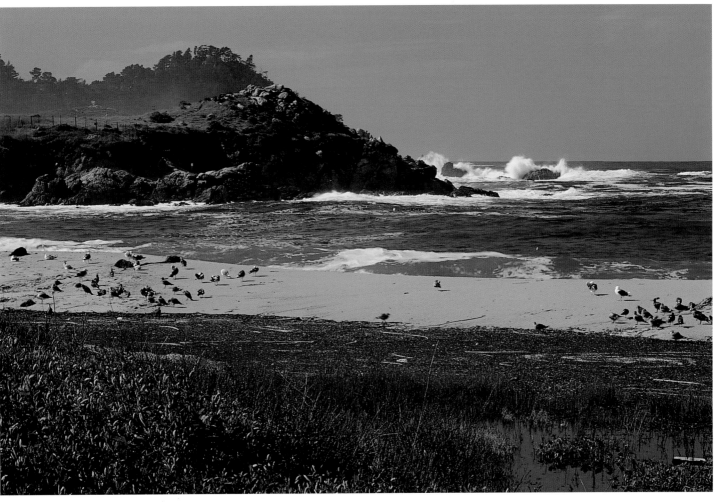

Left: The sweeping edge of the Bixby Ocean Ranch.
Above (both photos): American avocet and other shorebirds use
habitat provided by San Jose Creek as it flows through
Point Lobos Ranch to Monastery Beach.

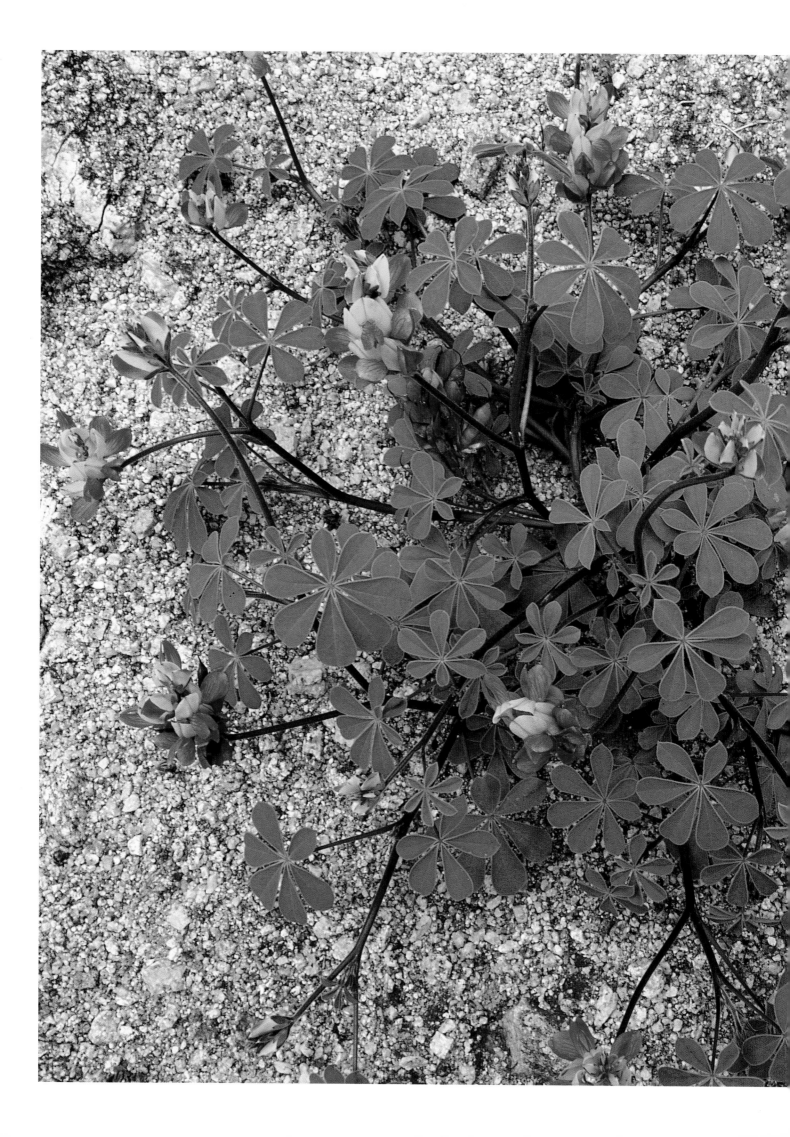

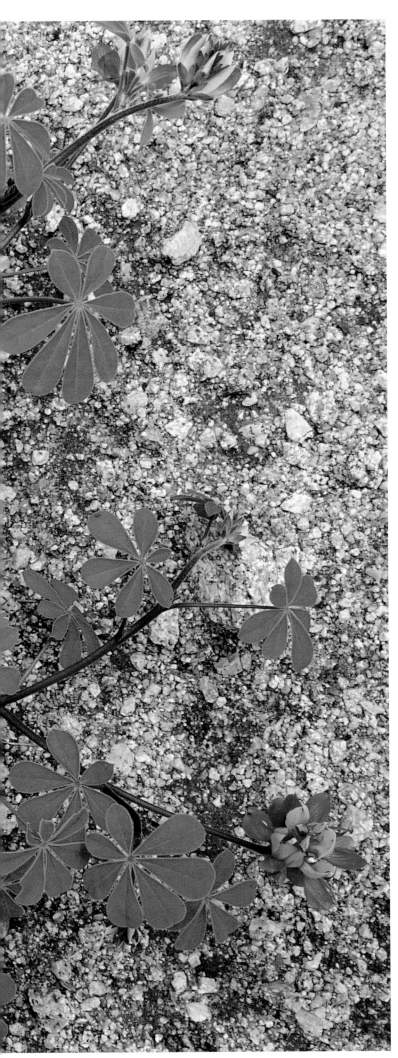

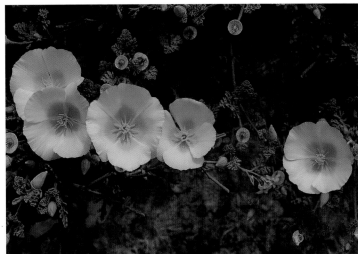

Left: Harlequin lupine in the Big Sur hills.
Above: The maritime variety of California poppies
along the Monterey Bay State Seashore.

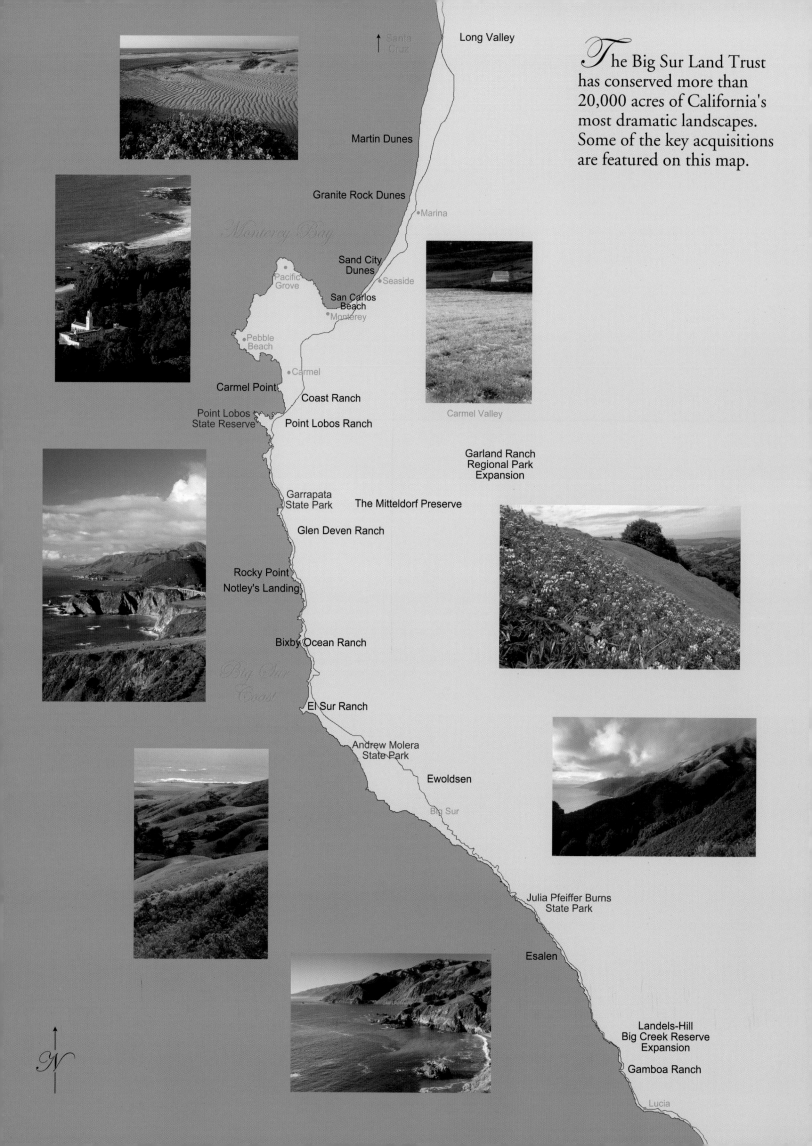

The Big Sur Land Trust has conserved more than 20,000 acres of California's most dramatic landscapes. Some of the key acquisitions are featured on this map.

Long Valley

Martin Dunes

Granite Rock Dunes

Marina

Monterey Bay

Sand City Dunes

Pacific Grove

Seaside

San Carlos Beach

Monterey

Pebble Beach

Carmel

Carmel Point

Coast Ranch

Point Lobos State Reserve

Point Lobos Ranch

Carmel Valley

Garland Ranch Regional Park Expansion

Garrapata State Park

The Mitteldorf Preserve

Glen Deven Ranch

Rocky Point

Notley's Landing

Bixby Ocean Ranch

Big Sur Coast

El Sur Ranch

Andrew Molera State Park

Ewoldsen

Big Sur

Julia Pfeiffer Burns State Park

Esalen

Landels-Hill Big Creek Reserve Expansion

Gamboa Ranch

Lucia

Santa Cruz

N

Acknowledgments

Douglas Steakley

DURING THE SEVERAL YEARS I have worked with The Big Sur Land Trust on this book, I have received support, encouragement, and assistance from many individuals. I would like to express my appreciation to all of them and, in particular, to those mentioned below.

From the beginning I received the full support of the staff and Board of Trustees of The Big Sur Land Trust. I would particularly like to acknowledge and thank Maggie Hardy. She was the first person I approached with this idea. She embraced it and we worked easily together from the beginning. Next, Stacy Dubuc and Zad Leavy, for the time and invaluable assistance they provided in a variety of ways. We have seen this idea develop from a conversation into a consuming project and a wonderful book. Corey Brown, the Executive Director of The Land Trust, immediately became fully involved and provided additional direction and guidance.

My trips visiting the various properties would not have been the same without the assistance and company of Nikki Nedeff. Together we have had some wonderful hikes and four-wheel adventures, not to mention a great helicopter ride up and down the coast. Both Nikki and I would like to thank Gene Richeson for sharing his helicopter with us on a memorable Big Sur afternoon. Before Nikki there was Steve Bachman, who also took the time to show me many of The Land Trust acquisitions.

There were many caretakers and property owners who guided me around their properties and pointed out areas I would not have discovered on my own. In particular, I would like to thank Bob Milton of the Gamboa Ranch, Gary Collings and Lynn Overtree of the Palo Corona Ranch, John and Suzy Moon of the Bixby Ocean Ranch, Jim Cox of the Glen Deven Ranch, Lloyd Addleman, and Jeff Norman.

I want to thank Mary Ransome, Tim Frew, Betty Watson, Jean Andrews, and the staff at Graphic Arts Center Publishing Company for making this book a reality. Graphic Arts Center Publishing® provided the experience and professionalism we sought in a publisher.

Most importantly, I want to thank my wife, Jackie, for assuming responsibility of our Carmel gallery so I could spend hours driving up and down the coast, visiting new locations and taking numerous photographs. Next, my daughter, Nicole, for her gracefully accepting that the days I took for hiking around in the woods were days taken away from our time together. It was a difficult exchange, since the years with a teenage daughter are precious and fleeting.

Last, but certainly not least, I would like to thank May Waldroup of Thunderbird Books. May is always the first person I turn to with questions about books and publishing. She has provided guidance, insight, and support, not only to me but to a large group of artists, poets, writers, and photographers on the Monterey Peninsula for many years. She is an inspiration.

Acknowledgments

The Big Sur Land Trust

THE BIG SUR LAND TRUST gratefully acknowledges those who made this tremendous legacy possible:

Zad Leavy, our Founder, General Counsel, and past Executive Director, whose vision, creativity, and dedication have been central to our successes.

Our additional Founders Pat and Lloyd Addleman, Peter Harding, Nancy and Sam Hopkins, Martin Forster, Suzann Forster, Laela Leavy, Beverly and Roger Newell, and Sherna Stewart who built the foundation for our conservation work.

David and Lucile Packard who made our first project possible, and for their vision in endowing the David and Lucile Packard Foundation, which continues to be a national leader in conservation philanthropy.

Dr. Seeley and Mrs. Virginia Mudd for their gift of the Glen Deven Ranch, Harriet and Arthur Mitteldorf for the preservation of the Mitteldorf Preserve, and Clint Eastwood and Maggie Eastwood for the donation of the Coast Ranch.

The Robert V. and Patricia Brown Monterey Fund, the Community Foundation for Monterey County, the S. H. Cowell Foundation, the Catherine L. and Robert O. McMahan Foundation, the Barnet J. Segal Charitable Trust, and The Turner Foundation for their special support of our projects and programs.

Our thousands of members and donors whose generosity continues to make our work possible.

Our elected officials, current and past, whose leadership has been critical to protecting our natural lands including U.S. Senators Dianne Feinstein and Barbara Boxer; Congressmen Sam Farr and Leon Panetta; California Governor Gray Davis; California State Senator Bruce McPherson; California Assembly Speaker Pro Tem Fred Keeley; Monterey County Supervisors Dave Potter, Karin Strasser-Kauffman, Sam Karas, and Lou Calcagno; the Monterey County Board of Supervisors and the Mayors and Councilmembers of the Cities of Carmel-by-the-Sea and Monterey.

Our public partners, including the State of California Resources Agency, the Department of Parks and Recreation, the State Coastal Conservancy, the Wildlife Conservation Board, the Department of Fish and Game, the Department of Transportation, and the California Transportation Commission; the United States Forest Service; the United States Fish and Wildlife Service; the Monterey Peninsula Regional Park District; the County of Monterey; the City of Carmel-by-the-Sea; the City of Monterey; and the University of California Natural Reserve System.

Our Honorary Advisors Clint Eastwood, Leon Panetta, Robert Redford, and Ted Turner for their continuing guidance and support.

Our nonprofit partners including The Trust for Public Land, The Nature Conservancy of California, the Monterey County Agricultural and Historical Land Conservancy, the Elkhorn Slough Foundation, Save the Redwoods League, the Ventana Wilderness Society, and others.

More than one hundred landowners who worked with us to preserve their natural lands.

Douglas Steakley for his incredible talent, generosity, and belief in our work.

Tim Frew, Mary Ransome, Betty Watson, and Jean Andrews of Graphic Arts Center Publishing Company for shepherding us through the publication process.

Our Trustees, staff, special friends and volunteers, past and present, and to our supporters worldwide who make the work of The Big Sur Land Trust possible.